The Individualized System

Student Participation in Decision-Making

William E. Alexander and Joseph P. Farrell

Ministry of Education, Ontario,
Library/Information Centre,
13th Floor, Mowat Block,
Queen's Park, Toronto 182, Ontario

The research reported in this book was funded
by the Ministry of Education, Ontario.

H.S.1 STUDIES

The Ontario Institute for Studies in Education

To Professor George Raymond Geiger

THE ONTARIO INSTITUTE FOR STUDIES IN EDUCATION has three prime functions: to conduct programs of graduate study in education, to undertake research in education, and to assist in the implementation of the findings of educational studies. The Institute is a college chartered by an Act of the Ontario Legislature in 1965. It is affiliated with the University of Toronto for graduate studies purposes.

The publications program of The Ontario Institute for Studies in Education has been established to make available information and materials arising from studies in education, to foster the spirit of critical inquiry, and to provide a forum for the exchange of ideas about education. The opinions expressed should be viewed as those of the contributors.

© The Ontario Institute for Studies in Education 1975
252 Bloor Street West, Toronto, Ontario M5S 1V6

All rights reserved. No part of this publication may be reproduced in any form without permission from the publisher, except for brief passages quoted for review purposes.

ISBN 0-7744-0112-5   Printed in Canada

1 2 3 4 5 6   MD   08 97 87 77 67 57

Contents

Foreword / v

Acknowledgments / vii

Chapter 1   The Need for Student Participation in Decision-Making / 1

2   Patterns of Influence / 33

3   Student Government Effectiveness / 57

4   Student Government as a Pedagogical Tool: What Do the Members Learn? / 79

5   The House System / 91

6   Summary, Conclusions, and Recommendations / 109

List of Tables

Table		
	1	Percentages of Students, Student Government Members, and Teachers Who "Don't Know" How Much Influence Is Exerted on Various School Decision Areas, Averaged Across Influentials / 37
	2	Percentages of Students, Student Government Members, and Teachers Who "Don't Know" How Much Influence Is Exerted by Various Potential Influentials, Averaged Across 10 School Decision Areas / 37
	3	Average Principal, Student, Student Government Member, and Teacher Ratings of Student Government Influence in Various School Decision Areas / 38
	4	Average Principal, Student, Student Government Member, and Teacher Ratings of Student Influence in Various School Decision Areas / 41
	5	Views of Principals, Students, Student Government Members, and Teachers on Desired Increases or Decreases in Student Influence in Various School Decision Areas / 43
	6	Views of Principals, Students, Student Government Members, and Teachers on the Best Way for Students to Participate in Decision-Making in Various School Decision Areas / 46–47
	7	Opinions of Students and Student Government Members on Various School Rules and Policies / 50
	8	Views of Students and Student Government Members on What Most Needs Changing in Their School / 51
	9	Correspondence Between Student Government Members' Degree of Desire for Increased Student Influence and Students' Levels of Dissatisfaction in Various School Decision Areas / 52
	10	Views of Student Government Members, Students, and Principals on the Ministry of Education's Influence in Various School Decision Areas / 54
	11	Student Government Member, Student, and Teacher Rankings of Schools in Terms of Student Government Effectiveness / 60
	12	Percentage Agreement of Student Government Member or Student Responses and Teacher Responses to Student Government Effectiveness Criteria in Schools Rated As Highest and Lowest in Effectiveness / 61
	13	Responses of Student Government Members in Schools With and Without a House System to Questions Supporting the King-Warren House System Argument / 106

Foreword

In the years between 1969 and 1973 an increasing proportion of Ontario secondary schools were adopting a new form of organization known as the "individualized system" or the "credit system." First offered as an option in the Ministry of Education's Circular H.S.1 for 1969/70, it was ultimately made mandatory in the 1972/73 school year. Since this scheme constituted a substantial change both in practice and in philosophy, the Ministry early on had formulated a number of questions concerning its implementation and its main effects. It was these questions that formed the basis for a number of research contracts with the Ontario Institute for Studies in Education during 1972/73. The specific studies sought to clarify the extent to which implementation of the letter and the spirit of Circular H.S.1 (1972/73) had taken place, and to identify the effects both direct and indirect of the changes.

The study reported in this book was not formally part of this group of contracts, in that it was separately funded by the Ministry of Education under a Grant-in-Aid of Educational Research. However, this project was linked with the H.S.1 contracts because it touched upon or complemented many of the themes central to the contract studies, and therefore its results are being published as part of the H.S.1 series.

The first report, by Dr. W. G. Fleming, presents an overview of the findings of the entire group of H.S.1 studies supported by the Ministry, and at the same time relates findings from two or more studies tending to throw light on the same question. Other titles in the series (including the present report) present in detail the results and discussions pertaining to specific topics of investigation. Acknowledgement is here due to the Ministry of Education for its support of the research upon which all of these reports are based.

It is important to realize that, although the various teams of researchers began by defining fairly distinct areas of investigation, they agreed that there should be some overlap. This feature of the work is of special significance to researchers because it is a readily accessible mechanism in group studies of this type, where confirmation of educational research findings is especially desirable. In most instances of overlap in the current studies, there is confirmation across studies and hence some added confidence in the conclusions. In cases where the appearance of conflict emerges, there are new insights into a problem that would be only partially dealt with, if at all, by a single research probe.

William E. Alexander and Joseph P. Farrell, the authors of this report, are both Associate Professors in the Department of Educational Planning, The Ontario Institute for Studies in Education.

Acknowledgments

The study upon which this book is based was funded by a Grant-in-Aid of Educational Research from the Ministry of Education, Ontario. We are grateful to the Ministry for its support of this effort.

Thanks are also due to Michael Schulman, formerly on the staff of the Office of the Coordinator of Research and Development Studies at OISE. His assistance in questionnaire construction was very valuable.

Jenni Gehlbach joined the research team as a research assistant after the study was well under way. She managed contacts with school officials and had responsibility for all phases of the data analysis. It can truly be said that without her the study could not have been successfully completed. Her work was invaluable.

A number of our graduate students were also involved in the work for this project at one time or another. The contributions of Norm Rowen, Jim Wood, and Lincoln Warner were especially noteworthy.

Throughout the study, we received advice and criticism from a number of our colleagues. Particularly important were the contributions of Ted Humphreys, Bryan Elwood, Graham Scott, Brock Rideout, and Mel Robbins, all of whom are members of the OISE faculty. Len Chellew, who was serving as OISE's School Liaison Officer during the field-work phase of the investigation, was extremely helpful in putting us in contact with the many boards of education and schools whose cooperation was essential. He also brought us in contact with many student leaders throughout the province who provided us with valuable information and insights.

Our secretaries, in the early stages of the work Vicky Georges and Bev Viljakainen, and later Jennifer Silmer and Mary Yeh, kept us as well organized as possible (no easy task) and saw to it that material was typed and ready when required. Their skills have been critical, and their patience with us at times heroic.

The study could not have been completed without the willing and thoughtful cooperation of the many students, teachers, and administrators in secondary schools of Ontario who provided us with the information upon which this report is based. Although we cannot mention them all, we wish to thank them all. There are, however, three administrators to whom we are especially indebted, Bruce Lee, Wally Beevor, and Charles Taylor. These men provided us with time and assistance, insights and ideas, far beyond the norm. Four secondary school students, Doug Coutts, Ellen Wexler, Robin McDiarmid, and Dan Wexler, also spent an unusually large amount of time talking to us, putting us in contact with other students, and reacting to material we were developing. We have learned much from these individuals, and from all the other students and staff members who have shared with us their understandings of the schools in which they live.

The authors of course are finally responsible for the conclusions and opinions contained in this book.

1

The Need for Student Participation in Decision-Making

Many books and articles that treat student participation in decision-making try to stimulate the reader's interest by discussing citizenship objectives and citing evidence – their own or others' – that these objectives are not being met through current arrangements. Such intellectual arguments apparently have not been sufficiently persuasive to motivate Ontario educators to examine seriously the area of student decision-making.

There is, for example, nothing in Ontario comparable to Sweden's SISK. SISK is a committee comprised of "representatives of associations of pupils, head-teachers, various teacher categories, caretaking staff, school welfare officers, parents, local school boards and the central educational administration"; it is concerned with developing "new forms of democratic association – often referred to as 'school democracy'" and with providing "functional participation" in the activities of the school.[1] There is nothing in Ontario comparable to the massive research efforts related to civic education conducted in Germany, Italy, Finland, Iran, Sweden, the United Kingdom, and the United States under the auspices of the International Association for the Evaluation of Educational Achievement.[2] And there is nothing in Ontario comparable to the Code of Student Rights and Responsibilities, published by the National Education Association in the United States, or to the NEA Task Force on Student Involvement, which developed the code.[3]

There are two points, however, that may provide Ontario educators with a greater sense of urgency. First, there is the argument that Canada's survival as a democracy may depend on the effectiveness with which secondary schools improve the organizational and decision-making skills of their students. Second, as Kenneth L. Fish said of United States schools, "To discuss the question of whether high school students should have power is an idle exercise. They do have it. This has been demonstrated again and again. The problem is that the power is being wielded by groups which are considered illegitimate and striving for goals which seem to be counter to those of the school establishment."[4] Today, most student power is exhibited in the form of student protests. And, as many Ontario principals have testified, student protests are very much a part of the Ontario scene. These two points are elaborated on below.

The Survival of Canadian Democracy
In December 1973, in an article in the *Toronto Star*, C. Northcote Parkinson offered this pessimistic prediction of our future: "During the coming decade there is one thing of which we can be certain and that is the continued decline of democracy."[5] He then described three steps that will transform democracies into dictatorships, a transformation that has already taken place in a number of countries. These steps are the centralization of power into one capital city, the placement of the police under a federal minister, and the limitation or abolition of all types of authority not derived from the central government.

Parkinson offered no advice on how this deterioration of democracy might be avoided. Indeed, he seemed to view such a transformation with a calm acceptance of the inevitable. He stated: "There is nothing rash about this prediction because the decline is to be expected in the nature of things and because, anyway, it is well advanced."[6]

While Parkinson may disagree, it would appear that Canada is in a uniquely strong position to counter this decline in democracy. First, Canada, unlike a host of other democratic countries, includes a number of provinces that jealously guard their rights and powers. Second, and perhaps even more importantly, there is in Canada a tendency to move further away from centralized authority by placing more power where the people are – namely, in the cities and, in some cases, even in the neighborhoods.

True, the current structure of Canadian society does not generate great optimism. While the urbanization of Canada has progressed at an extraordinarily rapid rate, the power of the urban centers lags far behind. In 1871, less than 20% of the Canadian population lived in urban areas, while today over 70% live in the cities. By the end of the decade, this figure will increase by an additional 10% to 15%. But the flow of tax dollars has not followed the population. The greatest share of tax revenues – about 54% – is claimed by the federal government. The provinces receive about 34%, while the remaining 12% goes to the municipalities.[7] Admittedly, at the present time the municipalities receive substantial revenues from federal and provincial coffers, but the control over these funds is, of course, vested in the government that holds the original claim.

The urban dweller of Canada is, however, beginning to learn, firsthand, about the political process and about his own efficacy. In several major Canadian cities, a boom in citizen participation is currently under way. Individuals who once believed that the only way they could, or ought to, influence city hall was through casting a ballot are realizing that it is more effective to exert influence on particular issues than to wait for an election and then try to organize for the defeat of an incumbent. Ratepayers and other citizen groups are developing their own brand of lobbying. Moreover, city hall is becoming receptive to the idea.

In Toronto, for example, the residents of the Moore Park neighborhood recently petitioned the city to erect barricades in order to stop through-traffic from using specific residential streets. The city agreed to implement the Moore Park plan for a six-month test period. Initially, the barricades created chaos in the traffic pattern: buses ran late, cars were tied up for blocks, and letters from irate motorists filled the editorial pages of Toronto newspapers. Eventually, the plan was cancelled before the end of the trial period; but by that time the idea of neighborhoods planning for themselves had taken hold. Groups from other neighborhoods began to submit their own residential traffic plans – within a few weeks, the city had received more than two dozen submissions.

As well as stimulating citizen involvement, the Moore Park experiment has generated substantial debate. Citizens are now beginning to gain some understanding of planning principles (or their absence) and are beginning to consider one of the most important and complex issues of political life: which jurisdiction *should* have authority to decide a particular issue?

Toronto is not the only urban center where citizen influence is invading city hall. In Vancouver, the Electors' Action Movement was instrumental in the 1972 election of a reform council. In Calgary, newly elected Mayor Rod Sykes has come down hard on what some have referred to as "bulldozer politics" and has sided with the Inglewood Community Association (against the city planning office) in order to save its neighborhood. Even Canadian cities that perpetuate aloof city councils are generating action groups, pressure groups, and other types of voluntary organizations.

The "responsiveness" of city hall to citizen groups has been severely criticized in some circles. There are those who claim that the incessant need by some aldermen to take all of the issues to the people is essentially an abdication of responsibility and has in some cases led to near-paralysis of the decision-making process. Other critics have argued that citizen participation is worthwhile, provided it is equitable. The problem, however, is that the rich have always had access to governments, while the poor never have. The broadening of participation simply gives the near-rich more bargaining power, thereby placing the poor at an even greater disadvantage in fighting for scarce resources. There are also those who argue that the so-called neighborhood groups are often self-selected subgroups who have no legitimate claim to represent the entire neighborhood.

Whether or not the reform councils of Canadian cities can meet these objections remains to be seen. All the arguments do have merit in specific cases, but none represents an insoluble problem and, more importantly, none contradicts the ideology of delegating specific, well-chosen authority to neighborhoods. The problem is whether or not the solutions can be implemented.

City councils are not the only focus of citizens' pursuit of additional influence. University of Toronto law professor M. J. Trebilcock suggests that there are many indications that citizens are beginning to focus on the performance of service industries and especially the professions.[8] He pointed out these facts:
1. The 1973 Pickering report commissioned by the Ontario Medical Association found that more than 75% of the people surveyed had serious complaints about doctors.
2. In Quebec, the Prevost Commission (1969) found that a majority of citizens who were surveyed had negative attitudes about lawyers. More recently, former federal Minister of Urban Affairs Ron Basford has charged that inflated legal fees constitute a significant factor in the high cost of house purchases. Lawyers also have come under attack for the high fees they charge for uncontested divorces.

3. Many citizens in Ontario have attacked both dentists and former provincial Health Minister Richard Potter for initiating legislation that eliminates denturists as an independent profession. The claim is that dentists want to monopolize the lucrative denture field.

The list goes on and on. Funeral directors are accused of fee-gouging and grocery stores of double-pricing. In Ontario, Imperial Optical finally lost its dominance over the Board of Opthalmic Dispensers and, presumably, its monopoly over the sale of eyeglasses when the province finally decided to appoint a majority of independents to the board.

Professor Trebilcock pointed out that the Castonguay Commission in Quebec, the McRuer Commission in Ontario, and a select committee in Alberta have all recognized the importance of evolving a master policy in relation to the professions. One key issue revolves around "public participation in the government of the professions, e.g., should there be public participation in professional decision-making processes pertaining to right of entry, fee-setting and disciplinary proceedings? How extensive should this participation be and what are the appropriate structures for it?"

A more humble request for involvement in decision-making was reported in a recent article in *U.S. News & World Report*.[9] The President of General Motors was becoming increasingly concerned with talk of worker dissatisfaction. He hired the prestigious University of Michigan Institute for Social Research to investigate the nature and extent of this dissatisfaction. The research team reported that the major concern of workers was their lack of involvement in the business. According to G.M.'s President, "they wanted to be asked what we thought about maybe building a cushion in a certain way or how we assemble something in a certain way. They wanted to be treated like human beings." The workers simply wanted access to decision-makers so they could pass on ideas and thereby influence decisions that would improve the manufacturing process.

Perhaps the strongest indicator of the movement toward public participation in decision-making is the ease with which we have been able to collect examples for this book. Newspapers and magazines are continually carrying stories of one or another citizen group fighting over some issue, of attacks by consumers on some profession or service industry, or of a voluntary association pressing the government for improvements in standards or enforcement of a pollution law. In addition, the vocabulary of public participation is being diffused throughout the land: "participatory democracy," "accountability," and "broadening the base of decision-making," not to mention such slogans as "power to the people."

The Educational Sector
Much of the impetus for, and many experiments in, democratization took place initially within the universities. Everyone is familiar with the events that took place in the 1960s at Berkeley, Columbia, and other major centers of higher learning in the United States. While protests in Canadian universities never gained the notoriety achieved by those within American institutions, we can claim to hold two dubious distinctions: Simon Fraser University in British Columbia holds the North American record for the number of university presidents hired and

retired in an 18-month period; and Sir George Williams University in Montreal holds the record for the greatest amount of property damage in a single protest. All of these events, publicized or not, led to experiments in broadening participation in university governance in Canada, the United States, Sweden, France, and many other parts of the world.

As we stated in a paper published in 1971:

> At one time public administration was a very mysterious process that could only be the responsibility of princes and properly sanctioned officials. The mystery has been swept away through a series of revolutionary and evolutionary steps toward democratization. As a result, public officials and politicians can expect neither to be free of criticism for long, nor even to be secure in their office. Similarly, until a very few years ago, policy making for institutions of higher learning was an esoteric, mysterious process that even the majority of professors could not hope to fathom, to say nothing of students, support staff and laymen. For better or for worse, the running of universities and other educational institutions has now been reduced to a mundane set of activities that associate professors, stenographers and students "understand" very well. No administrator, no scholar, no governor can expect to achieve such status that his judgements will be accepted in all cases. He may never expect that his administrative abilities or his political instincts will not be subject to criticism.[10]

Involvement in university decision-making is now moving beyond student and faculty participation. As stated in the *Draft Report* of the Commission on Post-Secondary Education in Ontario: "It should also be pointed out that increased faculty and student participation at the institutional level must be accompanied by more concerted efforts of the lay and public representatives to scrutinize the demands of faculty and students."[11] Accrding to *University Affairs*, the Manitoba task force on postsecondary education has, as one of its key recommendations, "the establishment of a decentralized regional organization, through which the needs of each local community would be decided by the people in that community and not imposed on them by a central system."[12]

All this new activity suggests a demand for increasing numbers of skilled decision-makers. The old model of the citizen in a democracy may be a thing of the past – that is, the intelligent, well-informed individual capable of wisely choosing between two or three candidates for a particular office. If Parkinson's prediction is to be proved false, then today's demands must be met: demands that require citizens who possess organizational and decision-making skills, understand the process of government and organizations, know how to obtain relevant information, and understand which decisions can be best approached through parliamentary debate and which are amenable to other approaches.

Universities have had the longest experience in democratization. But from our vantage point in a university, we are certain of one fact: most university professors are not very skillful at collective decision-making. From our own observation, and from the comments of our colleagues, we can conclude only that the decision-making process in the university, at least where professors are involved, is often inefficient, irrelevant, irrational, and sometimes incomprehensible. This situation, of course, is understandable. These experiments have been under way for a short period of time – too short for individuals to develop the necessary skills and too short for viable decision-making structures to have evolved.

The Secondary School
The traditional location for citizenship training has been the secondary school. If new forms of citizenship skills must be developed in order to prevent the realization of Parkinson's prediction, the secondary schools must assume a large portion of responsibility. Current trends toward decentralized decision-making with increased public participation imply that society will require vast numbers of individuals who possess organizational and decision-making skills. The secondary schools play two vital roles. First, they can provide students with the opportunity to develop collective decision-making skills – skills that apparently are sadly lacking, not only within university faculties, but in most of today's adult population. According to the *Draft Report* of the Commission on Post-Secondary Education: "If the degree of institutional independence is not to be drastically curtailed and public accountability not translated into centralized control, such public participation must become more effective than it has been in the past."[13] The message seems clear: public participation must become more effective, or there will be centralized control and loss of institutional independence. While the commission was referring to the university sector, it seems likely that the message is applicable to many other areas as well, including the secondary schools.

A second role the secondary schools play also is vital to the movement toward participatory democracy. A student's experience with his student government is ordinarily his first encounter with representative government and collective decision-making. It is highly probable that his involvement in this process will contribute to the development of his general attitudes and responses toward the organizational and bureaucratic dimensions of the school. These attitudes and responses represent a critical learning experience. In a modern society such as ours, most individuals spend considerable hours working in, or dealing with, complex formal organizations, and what students learn in and about their schools as organizations may well carry over to their later life. Are bureaucracies, as many believe, inflexible, insensitive, inept, self-perpetuating monsters that impose themselves on the defenseless citizen? Or is it possible for ordinary citizens to deal effectively and constructively with city hall, the federal government, the telephone company, the local department store, or the trust company that collects the monthly rent? What students learn *about* school may be as important as or even more important than what they learn *in* school.

Ironically, secondary schools are at one and the same time potential training grounds for the participant citizen and among the institutions likely to be called upon as accountable by the participant citizen. It may well be that the effectiveness with which secondary schools discharge their training role will be proportional to the trauma they experience through changes in their own decision-making structure.

When this study was initiated in the fall of 1972, Ontario students, parents, and citizens were beginning to express some general dissatisfaction with secondary schools. Critics of the educational establishment such as Illich,[14] Reimer,[15] Postman,[16] and Holt[17] were becoming known by parents, principals, teachers, and students. The United States Coleman report,[18] whose main conclusions were interpreted by many as showing that differences between schools have little effect on what students learn, was receiving a great deal of publicity and was considered relevant to Ontario.

A number of alternative schools were being created, particularly in Toronto,[19] and pressures for reforming public secondary schools were arising in the Ontario Ministry (then Department) of Education. The nature of these pressures was reflected in the influential H.S.1 document, *Recommendations and Information for Secondary School Organization Leading to Certificates and Diplomas*, in which greater freedom of student choice was recommended through the implementation of a credit system with individual timetables. These two innovations reflected the general philosophy of the document, a philosophy expressed in the following terms:

Seeking an opportunity to relate more deeply to the individual student and to involve the student more actively in educational decision-making, principals and teachers alike are changing traditional curricular and organizational patterns. New solutions are being sought to new problems in our constantly changing society.[20]

Educational politicians also were beginning to sense and express feelings of unease and dissatisfaction. In February 1970, Barry Lowes, Chairman of the Metropolitan Toronto School Board, stated:

For too long, young people were not allowed to make any real decisions affecting their school life. They were harassed by dozens of petty rules, the reasons for which had long been forgotten. The guiding principle seemed to be to keep the students in line, to keep the lid on. So we sat upon 99.9% of the students because we were afraid of the 1/10 of 1% who were the disturbers and radicals. Students should have a strong voice in setting any rules governing them and their behavior in the school and they should have equal responsibility for seeing that the student body lives within these rules once they are agreed to.[21]

In October 1969, Alex Thompson, the Chairman of the Toronto Board of Education, stated:

Students should be given a greater voice in running Toronto schools to head off "violent unrest". The Student Council should have the right to review all rules governing student behavior. Students should also be able to publish their own newspapers, form social and political clubs and invite speakers from outside the school. Many experts feel that, unless radical and basic changes are made to our secondary school system, we will have a great deal more trouble and violence.[22]

Student Protests in the Secondary Schools

A theme running through much of the comment in the late 1960s and early 1970s was that if something were not done to improve life in the secondary schools, the turmoil that wracked the universities throughout the 1960s would plague secondary school administrators in the 1970s. In the United States, a growing body of research provided evidence of unrest in the high schools. *Education USA* reported that 18% of the United States' 29,000 public and private secondary schools experienced serious protests in the years 1968/69.[23] In a study of 27 secondary schools in Syracuse, New York, Stephen K. Bailey found that 85% had experienced some type of disruption between June 1967 and June 1970;[24] and in a survey conducted for the National Association of Secondary School

Principals in 1969 by J. Lloyd Trump and Jane Hunt, 59% of the high schools and 56% of the junior high schools reported that they had experienced some form of student protest.[25]

In Ontario, persons interested in the extent of student protests were forced to draw their conclusions from personal experience and newspaper coverage. A survey of Toronto newspapers revealed that 20 protest incidents in Ontario secondary schools were reported between the period of June 1969 and June 1972. To some observers, these and other reports led to the conclusion that Canada's schools were experiencing, or about to experience, disruptions similar to those of the United States. H. L. Willis, Superintendent of the Ottawa Board of Education, and G. Halpern, Director of Research for the same board, appraised the Canadian scene as follows:

Those who feel that campus unrest of such proportions [as in the United States] could never occur in Canada should consider the evidence. Two years ago, a student boycott of schools in St. John's, Newfoundland, kept over 2,000 pupils out of classes for several days. In St. Leonard, Quebec, a determined group of teenagers barricaded themselves inside a school, delayed the opening of classes, and forced a political retreat until their demands were met. Within the last twelve months, Ontario high schools have been picketed and walk-outs have been frequent – involving several thousands of pupils across the province when the Minister of Education announced the extension of the school year. In April, 1970, a student strike in a northern Ontario school district, supporting a demand for a French-language high school, reduced the attendance at a secondary school to one-third and emptied the classrooms of two elementary schools for several days.[26]

Other observers, however, with access to the same informal evidence offered conclusions similar to that of a principal interviewed for our study: "The newspapers are blowing this thing out of proportion. They are reporting a disproportionately large number of incidents in order to increase their circulation."

Typically, members of the educational establishment tend to view student protests with one of two opposing orientations. To some, usually those who are predisposed to change, student unrest reflects a shift in the values and the ideologies of youth. These individuals recognize the legitimacy of many of the students' grievances. They also tend to view student unrest as a positive sign in youth – as an awakening of political consciousness, a revolt against hypocrisy, and an active attempt to realize democratic ideals. To others, student protests are the work of a small minority of frustrated students, frequently manipulated by Marxists, Maoists, or Trotskyites (often from the university). These students are viewed as indulging in antisocial behavior in order to inflate their own egos.

Regardless of how one chooses to interpret student protest incidents, there are two points with which most agree. First, a student protest incident places substantial immediate pressure on the principal, who must decide how to deal with it. Second, such incidents create considerable pressure for change over the long term. If the incidents are large enough and sufficiently extensive, the pressure can be applied to any location of authority: a teacher, a principal, a director of education, a school board, or the Ministry of Education.

For all these reasons, in initiating a study of student participation in decision-making in Ontario secondary schools, it seemed important to assess the actual extent of student protest activity in the province, as well as the usual style of protest, and the issues upon which protests focus. Thus, in the spring of 1972, we mailed a two-page questionnaire to each of the principals of Ontario's 684 public, separate, and private secondary schools, requesting information regarding the extent and nature of student protest activity in their schools during the preceding three years. By the end of October 1972, replies had been received from 565 (82.6%) of the principals. The information supplied by the principals was supplemented with information obtained from questionnaires completed by almost 3,000 students in 37 schools from all parts of the province who participated in a later phase of the project (described in a latter part of this chapter). These two data sets provide a useful picture of the extent and nature of student protest activity in Ontario secondary schools during the past several years.

How Common Are Student Protests in Ontario Secondary Schools?[27]
Of the principals responding, just over half (50.9%) indicated that at least one student protest incident or demonstration had occurred in their school during the three-year study period. Projected to the total population of Ontario schools, this suggests that about 350 of the province's 684 secondary schools have experienced one or more protest incidents in recent years. Further, more than 20% of the schools experienced two or more such incidents. Looked at another way, these figures suggest that, on the average, students protested somewhere in Ontario about something every other day during the school years 1969–1972. Turning to the student responses, we find that almost one-third reported that they had experienced a protest incident while attending their school. This is a surprisingly high figure in relation to the principals' reports of numbers of incidents, since most students who were present for protests that occurred early in the study period would have already left school by the time the student questionnaire was administered (spring of 1973).[28] Clearly, student protest incidents have been widespread in Ontario during the past few years and the 20 incidents reported by the Toronto newspapers represent a serious understatement of the extent of student protest activity.

When confronted with data such as these, many educators in the province have expressed the opinion that the student protest movement may have been strong in secondary schools a few years ago, but that it peaked about 1971 and has been on the decline since then. The information supplied by the principals in our province-wide survey indicates quite the opposite. Not only have there been large numbers of recent protest incidents in Ontario secondary schools, but the number of incidents and the number of students involved grew steadily over the period 1969–1972.

Principals were asked, for each protest incident they reported, to indicate in what year it occurred and how many students were involved. In 1969, 23 protests were reported, involving 2,619 students. In the next year, 76 incidents occurred, involving 6,526 students. In 1971, 150 incidents occurred, involving almost 10 times as many students as two years before, 23,203. By the middle of 1972, when the principals' questionnaires were completed, there had already occurred 123 incidents involving 12,144 students. Thus, the number of students involved in incidents in the first half of 1972 was keeping pace with the 1971 figures, and the total number of incidents for 1972 may well have surpassed the previous year's figures.[29]

Events since the completion of the surveys suggest that protest activities are continuing to grow. For example, the document recently published by the Toronto Board of Education, *Students' Rights and Responsibilities*,[30] was the result of student initiative and pressure. In the fall of 1973, the Ontario Secondary School Student Union organized a week-long workshop focused on student rights and responsibilities. In May 1973, the staff and administration of La Salle Secondary School "bowed to student pressure and reversed an earlier policy decision that would have forced every student to write 'final exams'."[31] In October 1973, students staged a walkout in some Northumberland and Durham county schools to protest their teachers' refusal to take part in non-academic activities.[32]

A large percentage of protests reported in the press during 1973 was directed against the provincially dictated educational spending ceilings. In June, student council presidents representing 20 secondary schools in North York presented a brief protesting the ceilings to Education Minister Thomas Wells.[33] In September, 250 students left their classes at Emery Junior High, apparently to protest the ceilings.[34] In November, students from three Toronto high schools shouted their protests in front of the Legislature;[35] and a few days later, 200 secondary school students from North York and Etobicoke marched on Queen's Park.[36] The largest turnout reported in Ontario – about 17,000 North York students – boycotted classes on November 14, 1973, to "show they blame their teachers, trustees and the provincial government for what they call 'the deteriorating quality of education'."[37]

All of these incidents were reported in the newspapers. As we have noted, however, newspaper accounts capture only a small proportion of the total number of protest incidents occurring in the province. It seems quite clear that the student protest movement in Ontario secondary schools is not fading away; on the contrary, there remain large numbers of students ready to lead or join in a protest of one sort or another. This situation leads to a second question.

How Do Students Protest?
Principals were asked about the nature of the students' activity during the reported protest incidents. They indicated that students in Ontario have chosen relatively peaceful means of expressing their discontent. The most typical student protest activity is the circulation of petitions to gather signatures indicating student consensus and mass support of a particular point of view; in 41.7% of the total incidents, petitions were circulated. Although outright violence, destruction, or unauthorized use of school property seldom occurs, the potentially disruptive effects of student protests are demonstrated in the frequency of student walkouts and classroom boycotts, reported in nearly one out of every four incidents (24.1%).

The student responses, collected one year after the principals' questionnaires were completed, paint a different picture. Students were asked to provide information regarding the most recent protest in their school, and also regarding the one before that, if two or more had occurred while they were enrolled in the school. More than half of the students reported that the most recent protest involved such disruptive activities as staging a walkout or a strike, or boycotting classes. Correspondingly fewer (19%) reported that the incidents involved circulation of petitions, leaflets, newspapers, or questionnaires.

There are several possible explanations for this difference. Perhaps students are most likely to be aware of and remember protests that involve dramatic and disruptive behavior; or it may be that the more disruptive incidents tend to occur in larger schools. It may also be the case that styles of protest are changing from the use of less disruptive to more disruptive tactics. It is significant, for example, that the student responses refer to a somewhat more recent time period. Moreover, there is a substantial increase (more than 20%) in the percentage of students who report a disruptive incident (walkout, strike, or boycott) in the most recent protest as compared to the protest preceding it.

It may well be, then, that the era of sedate and non-disruptive protests in Ontario secondary schools is coming to an end. In comparison to their peers in the United States, however, Ontario secondary students still appear a relatively peaceful group. As far as we could determine, there has never been an incident in Ontario that parallels the one in a Cleveland, Ohio, school where the students "literally threw six clerks out of their chairs and took over the office of the school. They invaded the superintendent's office, sprayed Coca Cola in his face, and blew smoke at him while he awaited help from the police."[38] Apparently, such incidents are sufficiently common to have stimulated schools to plan for protests:

Most well-organized city high schools have emergency plans. These outline specific procedures for deploying the school's own staff for maximum effectiveness in gaining control and restoring normal order. The advantage of accomplishing this through the work of school personnel rather than police are clear: students are less likely to over-react, and there will be less unwarranted and damaging talk in the community. Many people feel that calling the police is like pushing the panic button.[39]

In many United States high schools, however, police or security guards are on constant duty to deal with student protest incidents.

What Do Students Protest About?
Principals were asked to identify the focal issue(s) for each protest incident they reported. About three out of every seven protests (43.8%) reported were concerned with what may be viewed as the "trimmings" of school life, as distinct from academic matters per se, such as dress and hair regulations, smoking lounge privileges, cafeteria service and prices, athletics, dances and other recreational activities. Of these, dress and hair regulations were the most frequent areas of dispute, accounting for one out of every eight protests (12.7%). To the professional educator, such concerns may seem trivial; but to the students, they are obviously important.

Academic issues were the next most frequent focus of protest. Out-of-school academic issues, such as teachers' work-to-rule policies, extension of the school year, or expansion of provincial aid to separate secondary schools, accounted for 23.2% of all incidents. In-school academic issues, such as problems with individual teachers, attendance or scheduling policies, teacher dismissals, course content, or grading and examination policies, were the target of 18.8% of the protests.

The remaining 14.2% of the incidents focused upon such out-of-school political issues as the Amchitka bomb test, abortion, pollution, and the Vietnam War. Given this small percentage, the claim that a radical, politically concerned youth "movement" exists is almost impossible to substantiate.

The student responses generally support this picture of protest issues. For the most recent protest in their school, 45.2% of the students reported that the issue involved was among the trimmings, as we have referred to them. Comparison of the most recent protest with the one before it, however, shows that there seems to have been a decrease in incidents involving dress regulations (our impression from case studies and conversations is that most dress code problems have been resolved, usually in the direction of less restriction), an increase in incidents involving other kinds of student privileges, and a marked increase in incidents involving provincial or national policies or decisions, although the percentages for the latter are still low (7.8% to 17%).

One of the most striking features in these data is the wide variety of issues that have sparked student protests. We were able to establish 21 separate categories of protest issues, each of which summarized several discrete but related topics. Students in Ontario appear to be ready to protest about any issue, big or small, given a spark or a catalyst.

While many university protests during the 1960s focused on unique, one-shot issues (such as Berkeley's 1964 Free Speech Movement and Columbia's efforts in 1968 to build a gymnasium in Morningside Park), substantial efforts were also put forth by university students to gain membership on decision-making bodies. With such membership and by working within the formal structure, students believed that they would be able to influence a broad range of decisions. At the University of Toronto, for example, student/faculty parity in the decision-making process was at one time the most salient issue on campus.[40] At the Ontario Institute for Studies in Education, there has been a steady increase in the ratio of students to faculty on most departmental and Institute committees.[41] In the secondary schools, however, very few protest incidents have focused on reforms or alterations in the decision-making structure. In fact, only 3.4% of Ontario secondary school protests revolve around issues of student government elections, powers, or policies.

The focus by Ontario secondary school students on specific issues (such as hair and dress regulations and smoking rules) may represent a stage in the student movement. The issues about which they protest are ones with which a large percentage of the student body can identify; solutions (or resolutions) can be easily formulated and success easily identified. Perhaps more importantly, efforts to gain more general and legitimized influence through membership on appropriate decision-making structures present some unusual difficulties for secondary school students, as compared to university students.

First, the secondary school system has a more complex decision-making structure than does the university. Often, neither student government advisers nor principals know the locus of authority for specific decisions (data are found in Chapter 2). One student government adviser, a teacher who had served in that role for several years, who was highly respected by the students, and who was eager to have students assume more responsibility, told us:

If I were writing your report I think that someone has to blast the Department of Education. . . . I think that what has happened to education in this province is absolute and complete frustration – and this would include everyone, from the principals to the trustees of the county boards; no one knows who has the power. I don't think principals or even directors of education know where the channels are. Nobody has power and nobody knows anything about what's going on. The Department of Education is producing a whole generation of frustrated teachers, frustrated kids and frustrated administrators. Everybody is just running in complete circles and nobody knows what they can do any more.

In universities, the ultimate authority over most policy and administrative decisions is located on campus, and the official or officials who have the formal authority are, relative to those in the secondary school system, easily identifiable. In Ontario's secondary school system, however, students often do not know if the final authority for resolving a specific issue rests with the principal, the board, the Ministry, or some other agency. In one school we visited, students had been requesting a smoking lounge for the past four years, and each year students campaigning for student government promised to press for a smoking lounge. When we asked individual student government members why they could not have a smoking lounge, we received a variety of responses. Some believed that the board had a policy against smoking in the schools; others thought that fire regulations proscribed smoking; a few indicated that a smoking lounge had to be authorized by the Ministry, while another group said the principal was to blame.

A second problem faced by secondary school students is the absence of appropriate decision-making structures within the schools. Many universities had elaborate committee systems and faculty senates prior to the student movement. University students could exert pressure simply to take over a number of seats that were previously assigned to faculty members. Most secondary schools do not have such a structure. Therefore, students have the additional problem of pressing for the creation of a totally new decision-making structure, rather than simply changing the composition of currently operating bodies.

Do Student Protests Reflect the Feelings of Most Students?
As noted earlier, a common reaction among educators, when confronted with data regarding student protest activities, is to claim that student activities do not represent the majority of students. They feel that activists are, in the words of one principal, a "minority of malcontents," often stimulated or guided by individuals or forces outside the school.

It is true that most students do not actively participate in protests. According to the principals' estimates, in any given year from 1969 to 1972, no more than 5% of Ontario's 600,000 secondary students were actively involved in protests. Of course, many had no opportunity to become involved, since they were in schools where no protests were organized.

The student data may present a more accurate picture of the extent of activism. We asked students to provide information regarding protests only if a protest had occurred in their school while they were in attendance. Thus, the respondents represented a pool of "eligibles" – that is, they had a real option of participating or not in a protest activity. Of these students, 23.3% claimed they planned, organized, led, or actively joined the most recent protest, and 25.6% reported being similarly involved in the preceding protest.

Even accepting the higher student-based estimates, the activists are clearly in a minority. Two questions then become salient. (1) Are the activists in any significant way different from their non-active peers? (2) Do the non-active students support or oppose the activities of the protesters?

To provide an answer to the first question, each student who reported that a protest incident had occurred in his school was asked to describe his own involvement. The alternatives were:
1. I helped to plan, organize, and lead the protest
2. I joined in active protest with other demonstrators
3. I was in favor of the protest but said nothing
4. I was against the protest but said nothing
5. I was in favor of the protest and said so
6. I was against the protest and said so.

On the basis of this information, students were classified as leaders and organizers (response 1); active participants (response 2); non-active supporters (responses 3 and 5); opponents (responses 4 and 6); all others (those who did not report a protest in their school). It was then possible to compare these groups on a large number of individual characteristics. For the sake of simplicity, in the following discussion we refer to both leaders and organizers and active participants as activists and compare them with all other students, except in a few cases where further distinctions are instructive.

Much of the literature regarding university student activists indicates that they are typically children of permissive upper-middle-class and upper-class families, that they are high academic achievers, and that they are generally uncertain of their educational and career goals. It is also argued that activists have more free time than non-activists. Given their popular currency, these areas are explored first.

Are activists the children of higher social status families? We have two indicators of family status: education of the student's father, and a family consumption scale, which indexes the presence in the family home of such items as various appliances, air conditioners, color television sets, encyclopedias, substantial libraries, and original works of art. There are no significant differences between activists and non-activists on either of these variables.

Are activists the children of permissive families? Each student was given a list of the following 14 subjects on which families often have rules for their teenaged children:
1. Time for being in on weekends

2. Time for being in on weeknights
3. Amount of dating
4. Going steady
5. Time watching TV
6. Going around with certain boys
7. Going around with certain girls
8. Eating dinner with the family
9. Using the family car
10. Using the telephone
11. Spending money
12. Clothes and hair styles
13. Going to church
14. Household and garden chores/duties.

The student was then asked to indicate (1) whether his family had a rule in each area, and (2) if they did have a rule, whether it was established by the parents alone or cooperatively by the student and his parents. Activists do not report significantly fewer rules in their families. They also do not report significantly more cooperation in establishing existing rules.

Are activists high academic achievers? Each student was asked to indicate his mathematics, English, and overall average marks in the previous year. There is a very slight tendency for activists' mathematics grades to be lower than those of other students, but there are no noticeable differences in English marks or overall averages. Moreover, activists are no more likely than are their peers to be in five-year rather than four-year programs (a distinction that, despite the introduction of the credit system, still has meaning for students).

Are activists less certain about their plans for the future? We did not ask students for their detailed occupational plans, since these may not have been very firm, particularly among the younger students. We did ask each student to indicate how certain he was about his occupational plans, whatever they might be. Almost identical percentages of activists and other students are very certain about their future occupational goals (28.5% and 28% respectively). Likewise, the percentages of those who are completely undecided are quite similar for both groups (37.4% and 34% respectively). We did ask about *educational* plans in some detail – whether students wanted to go to university, to some other postsecondary institution, or to work, or whether they just did not know. Although activists are slightly less likely to want to go on to some form of postsecondary education (63% as compared with 68% for all students), the "don't know" responses are almost identical for both groups (almost 25%).

Do activists have more free time to protest and demonstrate? It is sometimes suggested that activists are more free to get involved in protests – that is, they have more time available – because they do not work after school, they spend little time in school clubs and activities, they live nearer to the school (spending less of their time in travel), or they are older (and thus less closely supervised by their parents). We have information regarding several aspects of this question. Students were asked how many hours per week they worked for pay after school. On the average, activists work *more* hours weekly (5.4 hours) than do students in general (4.3 hours). Students were also asked how many hours per week they spent in school clubs and activities. Students in general spend an average of 2.6 hours weekly, activists slightly more (3.3 hours weekly), and leaders and organizers of protests much more time (5.9 hours weekly). To put this last set of figures in its proper context, it may be noted that almost identical percentages of activists and non-activists participate in at least one school club or activity.

Additionally, students were asked how much time it took them to get to school in the morning, and how old they were. On neither of these measures do activists differ from other students. Generally, then, activists appear to be busier, to have less free time, than non-active students, particularly if they are protest leaders and organizers. This is a common phenomenon, as expressed in the folk homily, "If you want something done, ask a busy man."

The factors considered in the preceding paragraphs are personal or family background characteristics of students, which are outside the direct influence of the school (with the possible exception of marks, although even these are likely to reflect a mixture of native ability and an academically motivating home background). Arguments that use these characteristics to help account for student activism generally suggest that the roots of activism are outside the school, that certain students are likely to become activists because they come to school predisposed toward protest, ready to be enlisted in whatever cause comes along. This style of argument shifts the responsibility (or blame) for protest activity away from the school, viewing the school simply as the arena in which outside forces contend. The data just examined give little support to this line of reasoning.

Are activists more dissatisfied with school? Standing in contrast to the outside forces explanation of activism is the line of argument that suggests that students become activists because they are intensely dissatisfied with existing conditions and are not prepared to believe that normal channels and mechanisms are able to change those conditions. There is a great deal of evidence that student activists differ significantly from other students along this dimension.

Students were asked to tell us what they thought of the rules or policies in their school in 11 areas, choosing one of five responses: very good, good, moderate (neither good nor bad), bad, or very bad. The areas they evaluated were:

1. School rules about dress codes
2. School rules about smoking
3. Other school rules, such as hall passes, where students may eat their lunches
4. School rules about outside speakers and assemblies, unofficial leaflets and newspapers, student meetings, and political rallies
5. The way courses are taught
6. The types of courses given
7. The way cafeteria service is handled
8. The way each student is assigned to (or permitted to choose) courses

9. The way students are disciplined
10. The way students are graded
11. The kinds of dances and social activities held.

In every one of these areas, a greater percentage of activists than non-activists rates conditions in the school as bad or very bad. The differences range from 3.9% for dress codes (where the absolute percentages are also lowest – only 11% of the activists consider dress code rules to be bad or very bad) to 15.9% for other school rules. The average difference across all 11 areas is almost 10%. Though not very large, the greater expressed dissatisfaction among activists is completely consistent. Moreover, substantially greater percentages of activists (in response to another question) feel that their school has many unnecessary rules and regulations (77.2% of activists as compared to 52.7% of other students).

In another question, students were requested to tell us whether they got a lot, some, very little, or no satisfaction from (1) school courses, (2) athletics or sports, (3) clubs, plays, and similar activities, (4) relationships with one or more teachers, and (5) relationships with the principal or vice-principal. Significantly smaller percentages of activists claim to get some or a lot of satisfaction in only two areas – school courses (62.5% as compared to 72.6%) and relationships with administration (20.1% as compared to 28%). In the other three areas, the differences are quite small. When protest organizers and leaders are considered separately from active participants, however, the differences in satisfaction are substantial. For example, 32% fewer organizers and leaders than other students claim to get some or a lot of satisfaction from school courses. Only in the area of clubs and plays is there little difference in level of satisfaction. Although these results are not quite as consistent as those cited in the preceding paragraph, they still show generally lower levels of satisfaction among student activists. It is interesting to note that when asked to estimate how dissatisfied other students in their school were with life in school, 35.4% of activists and only 20% of students in general believe that most other students are dissatisfied.

We asked students how they would feel if they had to leave school: 27.6% of the activists would not care, whereas 16.5% of other students express this opinion. Among protest leaders and organizers, the corresponding figure is 41.2%.

Students were asked how they would feel if they saw someone damaging school property (committing vandalism): 26.4% of the leaders and organizers say they would be glad, 8.3% of all activists express this opinion, while only 3.1% of students in general admit to feeling so negative toward the school.

In another question, we asked whether students found life in school exciting or boring (or neither): 38.1% of the activists find school boring, while only 25.7% of other students feel this way. Substantially more activists than other students also feel that students in their school are treated like children: 53.7% of activists express this opinion, while only 29% of their peers agree.

A few contrasting pieces of evidence should be cited. Activists are slightly more likely than are other students to state that they feel deeply involved in what goes on in their school, although the absolute percentages are very low (11.7%

as compared to 7.8%). Activists are more likely also to have had more than one conversation with their school principal in a non-disciplinary context (24.4% as compared to 16.8% – not surprisingly, the corresponding figure for protest leaders and organizers is 42.4%). Thus, activists do not operate completely outside the normal channel of communication with authority.

In general then, with a few noted exceptions, student activists seem more discontented than do their peers. They are more likely to think school rules and practices are unnecessary and bad, they get less satisfaction from all school activities except clubs and plays, they are more indifferent about leaving school, they are more supportive of vandalism, they are more likely to find school boring and to feel that students are treated like children.

Given that they have turned to protests and demonstrations in order to express their evident displeasure with school, one would expect activists to express less confidence than do their peers in the usefulness of student government – the main regular channel for student influence – as an effective means of getting things changed. We asked students whether they agreed or disagreed with a number of statements regarding student government in their school. These statements are listed below, along with the differences in responses between activists and other students.

1. The teachers and principal do not let students who strongly disagree with them run for student government in this school: 7.8% more activists agree.
2. Members of student government feel free to speak their minds rather than saying what will make the teachers or principal happy: 7.1% fewer activists agree.
3. Student government in this school has all the influence it needs to represent the students properly: 9.6% fewer activists agree.
4. Student government in this school is just a tool of the administration: 10.7% more activists agree.
5. Members of student government in this school can almost always get important changes made by working together constructively with teachers and principals: 22.8% fewer activists agree.
6. Student government can change school rules even if the teachers or principal are against the change: 1% more activists agree.

As predicted, the responses to all but the last of these statements suggest that activist students are more pessimistic about student government than are their peers. Complementing these data are the responses to another question, which asked for the *main* reason why most people became members of student government. The possible responses were:

1. To get experience and a good record that will help later in life
2. To become well known and respected in the school
3. To serve the school and help it run smoothly
4. To cause important changes in the way things are done in school
5. To make themselves feel important
6. None of these.

Responses 3 and 4 can be thought of as indicating a service motive. Responses 1, 2, and 5 suggest a self-improvement or "ego-trip" motive. A greater percentage of activists than non-activists (56.2% as compared to 46.6%) selects a selfish or ego-trip motive as the main reason for getting into student government. Thus, activists are not only more pessimistic about the effectiveness of student government; they are also more likely to be cynical about the motives of its members.

Considering all the data presented above, one might expect student activists to be more likely to express a desire for greater student influence than would students in general. This is the case. Students were presented with the following 10 decision areas:
1. School rules about appearance
2. School rules about smoking
3. School rules about hall passes, lunchrooms, etc.
4. School rules about student political activity
5. Introduction of new courses into the school program
6. What courses students actually take
7. Disciplining of students
8. Evaluation of teachers
9. Hiring of individual teachers
10. Grading students.

For each category of decision, they were asked how much influence they thought students should have (responses ranging from none to a lot) and how they thought students should exercise their influence. Possible responses to the second question were:
1. Students should have complete control
2. Students, teachers, and principal should all vote
3. Students should give their opinions to the teachers and principal before the teachers and principal make a decision
4. Students should have little or no say.

For every decision category, greater percentages of activists than of their peers want a lot of influence, although in three categories (introduction of new courses, discipline, and teacher evaluation) the differences are very small. Similarly, more activists express a desire for complete student control over each decision category; the differences, however, are substantial – ranging from 7.1% to 20.7% – only where leaders and organizers of protests are examined separately. It should be noted that these differences relate to a rather conservative overall opinion set. In only two decision areas, excluding course choice (which the new credit system deals with), do more than 40% of even the activists desire a lot of influence – appearance rules (61.5%) and political activity rules (40.3%). Likewise, in only one area, again excluding course choice, do more than 25% of activists want complete student control – again, over appearance rules (29.8%). It appears that although student activists are generally more interested in a lot of direct student control of school decision-making, they are not as a group overwhelmingly committed to this goal.

It seems clear that activists are generally more dissatisfied with school than are students in general. Although the differences between the two groups are seldom very large, the pattern in all of the evidence presented is quite consistent and the exceptions are few indeed. We can now turn to the final question.

Do non-active students support the activists in their protests? To answer this question, we turn again to the responses to the questionnaire item, mentioned above, in which students indicated their own involvement in reported protest incidents. While relatively few students are active in protests, it is clear that far more students approve of protests than disapprove of them. For the most recent protest, 63.9% of the non-involved students supported the protest; 64.7% of the non-involved students supported the preceding protest. Activist students may be a minority and may be more dissatisfied than are other students, but when they translate their discontent into action, they have the support of almost two-thirds of their peers.

We began this introductory chapter by noting that students must be provided with the opportunity to learn decision-making skills if we want to preserve our form of government. To develop such skills, students must actually participate in decision-making. Motivation is just as important as is opportunity. On the one hand, a student who has the opportunity to participate in decisions he views as trivial may not be motivated to participate; on the other hand, he may be highly motivated if he perceives the issue as being very important.

In Ontario, over 90% of all secondary schools have some form of student government. This generally is the only formal structure that can provide an alternative to protest as a vehicle for change in the schools. In addition, virtually every school has a number of extracurricular activities. It is in these two types of traditional structures that students are assumed to have the opportunity to develop decision-making skills. They do not, however, seem to be working.

Increasing numbers of students in Ontario are dissatisfied with their ability to influence the decisions that vitally affect their lives during the many years they spend in secondary school. More and more of them are "voting with their feet," and most of the "silent majority" support the protesters. Response to this dissatisfaction is necessary to "keep the peace" in Ontario's secondary schools. More importantly, however, devising effective means of teaching students how to make individual and collective decisions, and indeed permitting them to discover that it is possible for them as individual citizens to influence political processes and large bureaucratic organizations, is essential to the very survival of Canadian democracy.

The Legal Status of Students in Ontario
We have observed that secondary school students in Ontario are increasingly turning to student protest activities as a means of expressing their dissatisfactions or airing their grievances. In this, they resemble their counterparts in the United States (and many other nations as well). There is, however, one important respect in which student protest in Ontario differs dramatically from that in the United States: the use of the judicial system to resolve disputes between students and individuals representing one or another level of the educational system.

According to Professor Mel Robbins, former director of OISE's Canadian Legal Education Project, in recent years students and parents in the United States may have filed several thousand suits annually against boards of education, principals, teachers, and departments of education. A large number of these cases has involved questions of students' civil rights – the legal authority of the school to impose various kinds of constraints on student behavior. Some of the cases have involved very specific questions. For example, in Tinker v. Des Moines School District, the court declared that students had the right to don a black armband to protest the Vietnam War.[42] In other cases, more general principles of law are at issue or are appealed to by the court in its decision. For example, in the case of Antonelli v. Hammond, where the right of free speech for students was at issue, the court declared:

The state is not necessarily the unrestrained master of what it creates and fosters. Thus in cases concerning school-supported publications or the use of school facilities, the courts have refused to recognize as permissible any regulations infringing free speech when not shown to be necessarily related to the maintenance of order and discipline within the educational process.[43]

In a related case, Brooks v. Auburn, the court spoke out strongly against censorship:

Arbitrary action, uncontrolled by specific and explicit standards, is as clearly unconstitutional in this connection as in any other form of protected activity. The arbitrary acts of a censor cannot be tolerated; not because arbitrary power will be abused in every case but because of its inherent potential for discrimination against unorthodox views.[44]

In Sullivan v. Houston Independent School District, the court addressed the question of the severity of punishment imposed by a school district upon a student: "If the punishment could be this severe, there is no question but that high school students as well as a university student might well suffer more injury than one convicted of a criminal offense."[45]

In most of these cases, appeal has been made to the United States Constitution, especially the Bill of Rights, and the result of the many decisions has been the development of a substantial body of common law that helps to define the extent to which the provisions of the Constitution apply to students in schools. This is not to say that the Supreme Court of the United States or any of the lower courts have decided that high school students are equivalent legally to adults and therefore should enjoy the full protection of the Constitution. As Hillary Rodham pointed out:

The court has avoided taking the easy way with a flat holding that all rights constitutionally assured for adults may be extended to children. Instead it has carefully tried to carve out an area between parental dominion and state prerogatives, where certain adult rights can be extended to children under specific circumstances. The court has also tried to fashion modified versions of other rights.[46]

Although there is no formal and unequivocal statement regarding the rights of children, but rather an evolving set of principles and guidelines within common law, these cases do reflect a strong concern within the United States regarding the position of students under the law, a concern that was totally absent in the past. Rodham described the historical status of children as follows:

In eighteenth century English common law, the term children's rights would have been a non sequitur. Children were regarded as chattels of the family and wards of the state, with no recognized political character or power, and few legal rights. Blackstone wrote little about children's rights, instead stressing the duties owed by "prized possessions" to their fathers. Early American courts accepted this view.[47]

This evolving concern with the rights of children in schools has not been evident in Canada. While the United States is rapidly establishing a set of school laws based on students' rights and obligations under the Constitution, an official of the Canadian Civil Liberties Association reports that he is unaware of any civil liberties suits filed by Ontario students. The absence of such cases is probably best explained by the fact that most legal experts agree with the opinion offered by a Toronto Board of Education document: "The Canadian Bill of Rights apparently does not apply to secondary school students while they are in school."[48]

Presumably, the Canadian Bill of Rights does not apply to students because the British North America Act explicitly defines education – and school law – as the sole domain of the provinces. Section 93 of the B.N.A. Act states that "in and for each province the Legislature may exclusively make laws in relation to education." The Canadian Bill of Rights has the status of parliamentary legislation and therefore is subordinate to the B.N.A. Act. This fact does not mean that students are not protected against criminal acts by school officials. It does, however, appear to mean that the provinces have the exclusive right to pass on school law; hence, the Canadian Bill of Rights simply does not apply to students in school.

At the same time, the legal status of children, and particularly adolescents, outside the school has been changing rapidly. Many of these changes have created dilemmas for principals and other school officials. Ontario recently changed the age of majority from 21 to 18 years; and when this occurred, principals began asking such questions as the following:

1. Does a principal have the right to suspend an 18-year-old student who returns from lunch with liquor on his breath?
2. Can a principal demand that an 18-year-old who has missed a day of school bring a note from his parents?
3. Under the credit system, can an 18-year-old approve his own courses?

These questions are subsumed under the more general question of how the principle of *in loco parentis* applies to students who have reached the age of majority. The Ontario Ministry of Education has made some attempt to clarify the rights of 18-year-old students, but only with respect to specific actions. It has not, as yet, come to grips with the more general question.

The change in the age of majority is not the only change in the legal status of children in Ontario. For example, those 16 and 17 years of age are in an ambiguous situation as the government continues to define and redefine the status of youth in this age group. Recently, the Ontario government passed legislation permitting 16-year-old girls to apply for an abortion without parental consent, thus granting them a "right" that was previously denied to them. But what does a teen-aged girl learn about society when she recognizes that she can apply for an abortion without asking her parents' permission, but must ask her teacher's permission to go to the washroom? Does this situation teach her that she holds a dual citizenship, so that one institution in society provides her with important options while another institution – the school – treats her with mistrust? In some cases, principals have asked girls who are pregnant to leave school. Under present abortion laws, a teen-aged girl could be forced to choose between leaving school or having an abortion. There does not, as yet, seem to be legislation pending that would proscribe principals from asking pregnant girls to leave school, although it seems likely that pressure groups will soon begin to demand such legislation.

This combination of changes in the legal status of adolescents outside school and the inability to use the courts to settle issues and establish common law precedents creates substantial problems for students, their parents, and school officials. The difficulties arise primarily from the absence of two conditions that would result from the use of the courts.

First, a judicial decision establishes a general rule throughout a jurisdiction, a common standard by which individuals may guide their own actions and judge the actions of others. Lacking access to such a legal mechanism, students in Ontario must deal with each rule individually, school by school and board by board.

School boards function as legislative assemblies and judicial systems. They establish rules that prescribe and proscribe the acts of students while they are in school. If an infraction of the rules is observed, the principal is obliged to take appropriate action. There are over 100 public and separate school boards in Ontario, and each has a somewhat different set of "laws." Thus, what is legitimate and acceptable behavior in one jurisdiction may be a violation of policy in another.

This lack of consistency is further exacerbated by the fact that, where policies are not explicitly stated, principals have the authority to make their own rules. Thus, even within a single school board, different principals give different rulings on the same issue. For example, in one board area we visited, we asked a few principals whether or not they allowed 18-year-old students to write their own excuses for absences. One principal said, "Of course I do: I'd be a damned fool to do otherwise. If an 18-year-old wants to miss a day of school, that's his business."

Another principal in this board told us that he discourages 18-year-old students from writing their own notes. He informs them that they may write their own notes if they wish; but if they do, and they are ever in trouble with school officials, they will not be allowed to have their parents accompany them. The first principal saw his colleague's approach as intimidation and noted that, in his school at least, if an 18-year-old student were required to meet with school officials, he would be permitted to bring a lawyer, his parents, or anyone else he wanted.

The second missing ingredient in the Ontario situation is the inability to use the courts as impartial arbiters of disputes within schools. It is clear from the information presented earlier in this chapter that conflict does exist in the schools. It is also clear that the kinds of arbitration and adjudication mechanisms available within school systems are often unable to resolve disputes satisfactorily;

otherwise, students would not feel obliged to resort to protest. Peter F. Bargen, a former Superintendent of Public Schools in Alberta, wrote that the function of an impartial arbiter

> can be performed more acceptably by the Courts than by any other agency of government because of the institution of judicial "independence." Judges are made independent of most of the restraints, checks and balances, and punishments which govern other public officials. As Dawson says: "The judge is placed in a position where he has nothing to lose by doing what is right and little to gain by doing what is wrong; and there is therefore every reason to hope that his best efforts will be devoted to the conscientious performance of his duty."[49]

Variations in policies affecting students that exist between boards, and in particular between schools in the same board, combined with the lack of access to an impartial arbitration and adjudication mechanism outside the very school system against whose policies students are often struggling, have served as catalysts in the development of the students' bill of rights movement – an effort to formalize and institutionalize a set of rights and privileges for high school students. This is a widespread movement, as witnessed by a statement in a proposed Bill of Rights for high school students in North York:

> The movement for a Bill of Rights is not confined to North York. It is proceeding in Etobicoke, Hamilton, Ottawa, and other centers across the province. The Ontario Secondary School Students' Committee (a body representing all high schools in the province), the League for Student Democracy, and other groups have made similar and supportive representations directly to the Minister of Education. The New Democratic Party of Ontario, at its last policy and leadership convention, adopted for promotion a Bill of Rights for high school students. The education critic of the Liberal Party of Ontario has indicated similar support recently for such a bill.[50]

The documents thus far produced have been heavily influenced by the Canadian Bill of Rights and the United Nations Bill of Rights. They also contain a number of statements that reflect some familiarity with cases resolved in the courts of the United States. For example, Article 2 of the Bill of Rights proposed by and for students in North York reads as follows: "Every student has the rights of freedom of speech, freedom of assembly, and freedom of the press, all subject to the standards of Canadian laws applicable to the general public."[51] The justification for inclusion of this article says much about the status of students in Ontario secondary schools:

> Too many lives have been lost and too many tyrants have been toppled by those in pursuit and defense of these sacred rights for us to need argue their validity. In short, it is the undeniable heritage and birthright of all mankind to be guaranteed no less.
> That there is, in fact, great need to codify such rights, for protection in schools, is in itself obscene. That there is academic and social discrimination against critical opinion expressed by students in schools is shameful. That the content of our education has a pronounced economic and historical bias, and continues unchallenged, and even rewards acquiescence is unnerving. That neither students, nor their elected councils are free to organize topical assemblies or use public address systems during school hours, *or after*, without special permission from principals is contemptible. That political, topical or even service clubs, organized by students, for students, cannot hold meetings in schools let alone advertise such meetings, or the nature of their organizations, on school property without Board of Education or the principal's permission

is outrageous. That where these are allowed, staff sponsors must watch over them much like fortified baby-sitters is insulting to young adults and destructive of independence and responsibility. That student newspapers must suffer the humiliation of staff sponsorship, the stern muzzle of censorship, the suppression of free distribution, and the victimization of student contributors is plainly intolerable.

Yet all these things happen almost daily in our secondary schools. They virtually constitute the fabric of our in-school lives. They violate immeasureably the goals of a free society.

In this brief, as students, we do not ask for any special status, nor any peculiar exemptions. We simply maintain that registration in a school does not relinquish membership in society, nor the rights that do attend it.

And, of course, in asking that the standards of Canadian laws oversee the exercise of such rights it is understood that access to a fair and public trial with legal representation if desired, is part of those immutable standards.

The Board of Education must now come to grips with the problem of establishing the appropriate mechanisms for justice.[52]

The response to this document by the principals of secondary schools in North York also is instructive. It reads in part:

The Bill of Rights seems to create an antagonistic relationship between school authorities and the student body. This document could reinforce those in the community who are opposed to student involvement in schools and discourage those who are attempting to develop new attitudes and techniques which promote a true sense of student participation.

The fundamental principles and ideals listed in the Bill of Rights are held dearly by all principals in North York. In the past, when problems arose, a principal decided on the issues under discussion in such a way as to be beneficial to the majority of students.

Individual differences and rights have always been considered and protected, and it has not been the custom of principals to hide behind inflexible statutes and regulations. While there are some inequities and antiquated features in our school system, our student population cannot be regarded in any way as an oppressed or threatened minority.

A document, such as the one in question, presupposes an adversary relationship and detracts from the humanistic approach that one would hope to develop when dealing with students.[53]

While North York principals may be correct in suggesting that this proposed Bill of Rights "could reinforce those in the community who are opposed to student involvement in schools," it is useful to note that throughout the province of Ontario secondary school principals (but not teachers) favor substantial *reductions* in student influence over political activity rules in their schools (see Chapter 2). Regarding the argument that the introduction of an adversary system will detract from the development of a "humanistic" approach, which school authorities are seeking to develop with students, it may be observed that many who argue the need for a bill of rights do so precisely on the grounds that such a humanistic approach does not exist in the schools of the province, and that there is little evidence that it is developing. Note, for example, the low level of expressed student satisfaction derived from relationships with teachers and administrators, reported in detail in the following chapters.

In the city of Toronto, another student Bill of Rights has been proposed. It reads as follows:

Every student may exercise his or her right of free speech, press, assembly, and expression subject to the laws applicable to the general public.
1. Every student shall have the right to wear political buttons, arm bands and other forms of symbolic expression.
2. Every student shall have the right to distribute and receive leaflets, newspapers, and other literature provided that such distribution does not interfere with the normal carrying on of classes in session. This includes the right to distribute political, birth control or any other information. As well, every student shall have the right to post material in designated areas. Authorization is not necessary for distribution or posting.
3. Every student shall have the right to assemble peaceably, and to form organizations within the school. Neither authorization nor a staff advisor is necessary for formation.
4. Every student shall have the right to petition for redress of grievances.
5. Student publications shall reflect the policy and judgement of those students responsible without censorship or restriction on circulation. If such material is libelous or obscene, then ordinary law respecting the press will deal with any problems.
6. Every student shall have the right to smoke or eat outside the school building or in designated areas inside the building.
7. Every student shall have the right to determine his or her dress and hair including hats and armbands except where it is an actual danger to health or safety or where it violates the laws applicable to the general public.
8. Every student shall have the freedom of movement outside a subject class. This includes the right to refrain from staying in a classroom during a study or spare when a subject is not being taught.
9. Every student shall have freedom of physical contact. This includes the right to the outward expression of affection for a person which includes hand-holding, embracing and publicly accepted expressions.[54]

Although this Bill of Rights has not been formally adopted by the Toronto Board of Education, a booklet entitled *Students' Rights and Responsibilities* was issued by the board in November 1973, based upon the May 1973 report of a committee composed of board members and students. Between publication of the May report and the issuance of the booklet, the Toronto board enacted policies that: (1) established advisory committees (consisting of an equal number of staff and students) in each secondary school in their jurisdiction, to consider such matters as administrative, academic, budgetary, and extracurricular policy; (2) recommended that each school establish a staff/student editorial board to review all school publications; (3) established a grievance procedure for students who believe they have been unjustly treated; and (4) encouraged student councils to set up a staff/student forum to "advise how the student council should collect, spend and keep account of extracurricular student activity funds in those schools where student funds are not handled by students."

Thus, although it is sporadic, some progress is being made in establishing general principles that at least apply to all schools within the jurisdiction of a single board of education.

Regardless of the eventual outcome of the students' bill of rights movement, the few students who have worked on a students' bill of rights have learned extremely valuable lessons in decision-making. They have been forced to consider such complex questions as the following:
1. What are the relative advantages and disadvantages of securing a written

statement of rights at each organizational level (i.e., the school, the board, or the provincial level)?
2. What are the legal implications of having rights authorized at each level? What are the differences in the legal status of rights authorized at each level?
3. What mechanisms are (would be or should be) created at each level in order to resolve disputes?
4. What strategies are most appropriate for implementing a bill of rights at each level?

Students active in securing a students' bill of rights have also learned about their own powers of organization and persuasion and about that vast complex known as the educational system. They have researched the rules and regulations of schools within their own board and the policies of boards throughout the province; they have studied the education acts of this and other provinces; and they have perused documents from other nations and from the United Nations. They have felt the frustration of meeting indifference among their fellow-students and the joy of encountering students from other parts of the province who share similar interests and ideologies. Some students have sat with principals, board members, and officials from the Ministry and gained an appreciation of the problems and difficulties these individuals face. They have met officials in the educational system who are truly sympathetic toward their cause and ideals, and they have been confronted by others who view them as charlatans, trouble-makers, or deviants. While still in their teens, these student leaders have already learned more – cognitively and affectively – about the politics of education than their parents' generation knows after three, four, or five decades of naive and uncritical exposure to the educational system. If any curriculum planner could design a problem for students that would lead to a fraction of the learning that has taken place through the students' bill of rights movement, then that planner should feel extremely proud. The key, quite simply, is that to the students involved in the students' rights movement the problems with which they are dealing have a personal reality and significance that make them relevant, important, and therefore interesting.

The Study Design
In examining student participation in decision-making in Ontario secondary schools, we pursued two lines of activity. First, during the spring of 1972, two case studies were undertaken, involving intensive and extensive interviewing of students, teachers, and administrators. One was in a relatively standard traditional school; the other, in a "free" school. These studies were designed to alert the investigators to the kinds of questions that could usefully be considered and to give some sense of the range of possible responses to various questions. They also generated a number of useful early working hypotheses, which informally structured much of the rest of the study activity.

Second, a broad-ranging survey of students, teachers, and principals in Ontario secondary schools was undertaken. A stratified cluster sampling design was used to select a random sample of Ontario schools. The entire province was divided into two sections: the urban areas of the "golden horseshoe," extending from Oshawa to Niagara Falls; and the rest of the province. Schools were then selected according to a standard sampling formula within each region. The sampling ratio in the second group was twice that in the first group.

This stratification procedure was used for two reasons. First, many educators in Ontario have claimed that the golden horseshoe schools are different in many ways from those in the rest of the province. We wanted to be able to test this impression systematically. Second, we wanted to ensure adequate representation of schools in small communities and rural areas throughout the province. If a simple random selection formula had been used, these rural schools could have been swamped by the many urban schools in Ontario.

Once the schools were identified, a random sample of students in each school (approximately 7.5% of the students) was selected to complete questionnaires. Principals were given detailed instructions regarding the procedure to use in making the actual selection. We believe these instructions were followed in all cases. In addition, questionnaires were provided for all student government members in each school (except in a few schools with very large student governments, where a sample of members was chosen) and for all teachers. Each principal also received a questionnaire.

Once the sample schools were selected, permission was sought from the appropriate local authorities to administer the questionnaires in these schools. In most cases, permission was easily obtained; but an important pattern of acceptance and refusal developed. It was considerably more difficult to gain access to schools in the large urban areas of the golden horseshoe than in other parts of the province. Many education authorities in the large urban areas felt that their schools were being "over-studied," that they were being inundated by investigations. This reaction results, in part at least, from the proximity of these schools to the large universities of Ontario from which most educational research in the province is generated, and it may represent a serious problem for future educational research in Ontario.

In cases of refusal to participate in the study, an attempt was made to secure permission for access to a school adjacent to the non-cooperating school in the original sampling list. In cases where this was not possible (for example, where a board of education refused access to all schools in its jurisdiction, and adjacent schools were in the same board area as the original sample school), we attempted to substitute a school that was similar to the original sample school in terms of size and other characteristics. In most cases, one of these two substitution mechanisms was successful.

The refusals and subsequent substitution attempts created one substantive problem. More substitutions were required for golden horseshoe schools than for schools in the rest of the province. Thus, the deviations from the originally planned random design are greater among this category of schools. It was originally planned to have 28 schools outside the golden horseshoe and 17 within it. Data were eventually obtained from 24 schools in the first group (86%) and from 13 of the second group (76%). Moreover, those 13 included more substitutes. Thus, in interpreting the data reported in this study, it must be remembered that the actual responses obtained deviate from a fully random design.

The deviations do not, however, appear to be so serious as to vitiate the general patterns of the results reported. Indeed, our experience in gaining access to schools and getting usable data from them is considerably more satisfactory than is the norm for this type of survey research. This success may reflect a circumstance that we have observed from many informal communications with principals, students, and teachers – namely, that the subject of this investigation is a matter of great interest in the secondary schools of Ontario.

Of the originally planned 45 schools in the random sample, data were received from 37 and questionnaires were returned by 2,860 students, 846 teachers, and 843 members of student governments. On the basis of the original sample design, it was estimated that questionnaire responses ought to be obtained from an average of 80 students, 25 student government members, and 50 teachers per participating school. The actual figures were 78.5 students, 23.7 student government members, and 44.3 teachers per school. These figures represent an unusually high level of response for this type of study.

Outline of Report

It may be useful at this point to indicate the nature of the discussion contained in the following chapters. While each chapter asks a large number of questions, it is possible to identify the broad questions that we consider to be the most essential.

In Chapter 2, we ask: (1) How much influence do students have over decisions that directly affect them? (2) How much influence do students desire and how much influence do principals and teachers think students ought to have? (3) How do students, principals, and teachers think students should participate in the decision-making process (that is, in which decision, if any, should students share authority or play an advisory role, and from which should they be totally excluded?)?

Almost all Ontario secondary schools have a student government. Furthermore, in most schools, the student government is the only formal and legitimate organization through which students can voice their collective opinions and exercise influence. In Chapter 3, we examine the principals' conception of effective student government and ask whether or not this conception corresponds to the criteria of others within the educational system.

In Chapter 4, we examine the pedagogical consequences of serving in student government. This analysis asks two main questions: (1) Does serving in an "effective" student government provide more positive learning than serving in an "ineffective" student government? (2) What is the relationship between length of service in student government and a variety of pedagogical outcomes?

In Chapter 5, we examine the consequences of adopting the only alternative to traditional forms of organizing student participation that has gained popularity in Ontario – the house system.

Finally, in Chapter 6, we briefly summarize the need for and current state of student participation in decision-making in Ontario's secondary schools, and identify some of the factors that we believe to be major blocks inhibiting the development of student decision-making skills.

Notes

1. National Swedish Board of Education, *Partnership in School* (Stockholm: National Swedish Board of Education, Informationssektionen, 1971).
2. Judith V. Torney, "Civic Education, Political Socialization, and the IEA Ten Nation Study: A Progress Report" (paper prepared for delivery at the Symposium on Cross-National Studies of Political Socialization at the National Council for the Social Studies, Denver, Colorado, November 25, 1971).
3. NEA Task Force on Student Involvement, "Code of Student Rights and Responsibilities" (received by the 1971 Representative Assembly of the National Education Association and referred to its Executive Committee and Board of Directors for implementation, Washington, D.C., 1971).
4. Kenneth L. Fish, *Conflict and Dissent in the High School* (New York: Bruce Publishing, 1970).
5. C. Northcote Parkinson, *Toronto Star*, December 29, 1973.
6. *Ibid.*
7. Allan M. Maslove, *The Pattern of Taxation in Canada*, Report prepared for the Economic Council of Canada (Ottawa: Information Canada, 1973), table 4.1, pp. 48-49.
8. M. J. Trebilcock, "Making Professions Accountable to the Public," *Globe and Mail* (Toronto), January 4, 1974.
9. "Are Big Cars Doomed?" Interview with Edward N. Cole, *U.S. News & World Report*, LXXV (December 31, 1973), 32-36.
10. W. E. Alexander, *Patterns in Higher Education: A Case Study of an Educational Institute* (Toronto: Ontario Institute for Studies in Education, 1971).
11. Commission on Post-Secondary Education in Ontario, *Draft Report* (Toronto: Queen's Printer, 1972), p. 33.
12. Quoted in *University Affairs*, January 1974, p. 5.
13. Commission on Post-Secondary Education in Ontario, *Draft Report*, p. 33.
14. Ivan Illich, *Deschooling Society* (New York: Harper & Row, 1972).
15. Everett Reimer, *School Is Dead: Alternatives in Education* (Garden City, N.Y.: Doubleday, 1971).
16. Neil Postman and Charles Weingartner, *Teaching as a Subversive Activity* (New York: Delacorte Press, 1969).
17. John Holt, *How Children Fail* (New York: Pitman Publishing, 1964).
18. James S. Coleman, et al., *Equality of Educational Opportunity* (Washington, D.C.: U.S. Government Printing Office, 1966).
19. *Directory of Canadian Alternative and Innovative Education* (Toronto: Communitas Exchange, December 1973).
20. Ontario Department of Education, *Recommendations and Information for Secondary School Organization Leading to Certificates and Diplomas*, Circular H.S.1 (1972/73), p. 4.
21. Quoted in "Bill of Rights," a brief presented by the North York Citizens for Education to the Academic and Management Committee of the North York Board of Education, June 10, 1970, pp. 7-8.
22. *Ibid.*, p. 7.
23. "'Serious Protest' Found in 18% of High Schools," *Education USA*, March 2, 1970, p. 145.
24. Stephen K. Bailey, *Disruption in Urban Public Secondary Schools*, Final Report (Syracuse University, N.Y., August 1970).
25. Lloyd J. Trump and Jane Hunt, *Report on a National Survey of Secondary School Principals on the Nature and Extent of Student Activism* (Washington, D.C.: Department of Health, Education and Welfare, U.S. Office of Education, March 1969).
26. H. L. Willis and Gerald Halpern, "A Survey of How Students Perceive their High Schools," *Education Canada*, X (June, 1970), 29-33.
27. Much of the information on student protest contained in the following sections originally appeared in W. E. Alexander and J. P. Farrell, "Protests Grow for Student Participation in High Schools," *School Progress*, XLII (June, 1973), 22-24.

28. It must be remembered also that the two sets of data are not precisely comparable, since the unit of measurement in one case is the protest incident and in the other, the student. Moreover, they refer to slightly different time periods.

29. Some of the apparent increase in the number of students involved may result from a memory bias on the part of the principals. Principals are more likely to recall accurately recent protests and to forget some of those that took place two or three years previously. This, however, would likely be true only of small-scale protests involving very few students.

30. *Students' Rights and Responsibilities* (Toronto: Toronto Board of Education, 1973).

31. "La Salle Students Win, Final Exams Cancelled," *Globe and Mail* (Toronto), May 8, 1973.

32. "200 Students Remain Out in Cobourg," *Globe and Mail* (Toronto), October 25, 1973.

33. "North York Students Protest Budget Ceiling," *Toronto Star*, June 7, 1973.

34. "About 250 Students Left Classes at Emery Junior High School . . .," *Globe and Mail* (Toronto), September 15, 1973.

35. "Students Protest Against Larger Classes," *Globe and Mail* (Toronto), November 6, 1973.

36. "200 Students March in Spending Protest," *Toronto Star*, November 9, 1973.

37. "17,000 Students in North York Boycott High Schools in Protest," *Globe and Mail* (Toronto), November 15, 1973.

38. Fish, *Conflict and Dissent*, pp. 1-2.

39. *Ibid.*, p. 52.

40. Jack Quarter, *The Student Movement of the Sixties* (Toronto: Ontario Institute for Studies in Education, 1972).

41. W. E. Alexander and J. P. Farrell, "Who Are We and Where Are We Going?" An Analysis of Patterns of Development in a New Academic Institution, *Research in Higher Education* (forthcoming).

42. Tinker v. Des Moines Independent Community School District, 393 U.S. 503, 506.

43. NEA Task Force on Student Involvement, "Code of Student Rights and Responsibilities," (Washington, D.C.: National Education Association Publications, 1971) p. 27.

44. *Ibid.*

45. *Ibid.*, p. 29.

46. Hillary Rodham, "Children and the Law," *Harvard Educational Review*, XLIII (November, 1973), p. 497.

47. *Ibid.*, p. 489.

48. Board of Education for the City of Toronto, "Report from the Work Group on the Proposed Students' Bill of Rights" (Toronto, May 1973), p. 13.

49. P. F. Bargen, *The Legal Status of the Canadian Public School Pupil* (Toronto: Macmillan of Canada, 1961), p. 11.

50. The Inter-Collegiate Student Council for North York, "Bill of Rights for High School Students in North York" (presented to the Academic and Management Committee of the North York Board of Education, March 1, 1971), pp. 2, 3.

51. *Ibid.*, p. 9.

52. *Ibid.*

53. North York principals' comments on the proposed Bill of Rights, November 1970, p. 4.

54. Board of Education for the City of Toronto, "Report on Proposed Students' Bill of Rights," Appendix C, p. 1.

2

Patterns of Influence

Most of us who are over 30 years of age have mixed memories of our secondary school experiences, but there are few of the "over-30 generation" who have any recollections of student protests. While we may have felt uncomfortable about certain rules and regulations, and we may have criticized some of the traits of our principal, vice-principal, and teachers, any feelings of discomfort or annoyance were not articulated into issues about which we felt we could do anything. Perhaps, as some of our peers have suggested, our generation was too polite or too concerned with other matters; or perhaps, as other peers have suggested, we were too naive, too frightened, or simply brainwashed. But regardless of the reason, it simply never occurred to most of us that we could alter anything at all within the school, much less change the school system itself.

As the information presented in the previous chapter indicates, many students today believe that they can change the conditions under which they live. Moreover, they are prepared to articulate their complaints and act upon them. This view has, of course, resulted in increased pressures upon teachers and administrators. It has also produced increased pressures upon the one forum within the schools for expressing student views – the student government.

Many students are developing new expectations about the role their student government ought to play in the life of their school. Whenever such a transition in role expectations occurs, opinions tend to become more clearly focused and sharpened,[1] particularly the opinions of those people who are directly affected by such changes. Students, no less than principals and teachers, are affected by these role changes. Understandably, different students see their student government in different ways. Here are some typical comments about student government made by students who responded to our questionnaire:

The students' council in this school are a bunch of troublemakers, who go out of their way to force an issue with the "office." They have intense feelings of office prosecution. If they realized that one must work with the Principal and Vice-Principals they would get much more done. A large part of the student body dislikes the Council. As a result there is a feud running between my club and the students' council.

The reason why we have a terrible student government is because our president just isn't active enough and he always wants to be on the side of the kids. Because the student government is awful we have no school spirit.

I think that each year the student council is getting worse. We no longer have a large voice in things that go on. If there's any voting to be done the students' council does it. They make all the decisions. The student body is not considered at all.

Students do not have enough say in what goes on in student council. The activity director says the most and I don't think he should. He should give opinions and if we disagree then he shouldn't go ahead with whatever it was anyways. Votes should be taken by staff and students and whatever the majority says, that should be it.

I think that our school would be better off, and both the teachers and the students happier if the students had more say in the student council. The student council has no decisive power whatsoever, and all decisions are made by the principal or the student coordinator.

These comments reflect a variety of opinions concerning student councils. Different students characterize their student government as "troublemakers," "apathetic," "authoritarian," and "totally lacking in power." In this chapter, we look at the levels and kinds of influence student governments and students in general exert in secondary schools in Ontario, and at the levels and kinds of influence they (and teachers and principals) think they should have.

While Ontario's Ministry of Education has recommended greater student participation in decision-making, there is nothing in provincial law that requires any form of student government in the schools. In most cases, boards of education leave the entire matter to the principals. Thus, within the constraints of board policy, the principals are authorized to decide on the structure and function of the student government. In addition, most boards authorize the principals to decide on the kinds of issues to be discussed and the manner in which students are to participate in the resolution of these issues.

In general, there are three possible methods by which the student government may influence decisions: persuasion, authority, and pressure tactics. First, and most commonly, it has access to the principal, through regularly scheduled meetings, through an "open office policy," or through the adviser to student government. Access is a prerequisite for communication and persuasion, although, of course, there is no guarantee that the principal will be receptive to the ideas proposed by the student government. In one Ontario school, the principal frankly informed us that he "always" gives more weight to the advice or arguments of his department heads than to students' comments. He did not even give the pretense of placing greater weight on the idea that had the greatest virtue. For him, the source of the idea, not its intrinsic merit, was the important factor.

A second possible method for exerting influence is through the exercise of authority that has been delegated to the student government by the principal. Once a principal has delegated authority to the student government, this body can make or participate in decisions by virtue of the legitimate authority it possesses.

A third method used by some student governments for exerting influence is pressure tactics. Presenting the principal with a petition signed by students or parents, organizing students in a school boycott, and releasing stories to newspapers are some of the strategies that have been used. A principal's perception of the student government's motivation and ability to use such tactics directly affects his view of its influence. In one school we visited, the student government had been pleading with the principal for permission to let the girls wear slacks to school, but the principal had consistently refused. Finally, some student government (SG) members decided to circulate petitions. These petitions, signed by a large number of students and parents, were presented to the principal; and in response, the principal decided on a test period during which girls would be allowed to wear slacks. At the end of the test period, nothing was said. Two years have now passed since the termination of the test period, the principal has made no statement on the "legality" of wearing slacks, and the girls continue to wear them to school.

It should be noted that an *individual* student also may have influence, whether or not he is an SG member. His effectiveness may be attributed to one of several circumstances:

1. He may possess some personal attributes that have resulted in his developing a personal relationship with the principal. This is a trust relationship.
2. He may be perceived by the principal as a leader in molding the opinions of students and directing their activities (for example, a student activist leader). This is a power relationship.
3. He may possess legitimate authority, delegated to him by an office superior to the principal's. H.S.1, for example, gave students the right to choose a variety of courses that at one time were subject to the principal's decision.[2]
4. He may possess specialized information and legitimate authority delegated to him within the school. A team captain on the playing field often has this kind of influence, depending upon how much authority the coach has delegated to him.

There is no generally accepted method available that permits one to describe accurately the structure of influence within the school system, much less the degree of influence that students and student governments possess.[3] The closest approximation may be perceptions of influence, both by students and SG members and by principals and teachers.

Power may be defined as the "potential ability of an actor or actors to select, to change and to attain the goals of a social system."[4] Influence, according to this definition, is "the exercise of power that brings about change in a social system."[5] Thus, the principal's perception of the influence of the student government is determined by his perception of the degree to which it exercises power. The student government's perception of its influence reflects its belief about the degree of power it exercises. The principal who perceives the student government as having a great deal of power over certain decision areas tends to behave differently from the one who believes it has very little power. And, of course, a student government that is aware of its power – and knows that the principal also is aware – is probably more aggressive in pressing for particular policies or reforms.

The educational system consists of a large number of decision-making structures. These structures vary in relationship to specific classes of decisions. For example, there exists a class of decisions in which the Ministry of Education exercises its authority directly, allowing principals no formal participation rights. In other classes of decisions, the principal assumes final authority; here, teachers and students may influence decisions, but only in an informal way.

Because in our study we were concerned primarily with students' perceptions of decision-making structures, we conceptualized the components (that is, the potential influentials) of the decision-making structure(s) in a way familiar to students, as follows:
1. The Ontario Ministry of Education
2. The board of education, the director of education, or the superintendent(s)
3. The principal or vice-principal(s)
4. The teachers
5. The SG members
6. The students in general
7. Your close friends
8. You yourself.

Respondents' perceptions of influence were obtained for the following 10 decision areas:
 1. School rules about appearance, such as dress codes and hair styles
 2. School rules about smoking
 3. Other school rules, such as hall passes, where students may eat their lunches
 4. School rules about student political activities (concerning internal as well as external issues), such as the use of the school for outside speakers and assemblies, newspapers, unofficial leaflets, student meetings, political rallies
 5. Introduction of new courses not previously included in the school program
 6. What courses students actually take
 7. Disciplining of students
 8. Evaluation of teachers
 9. Decisions regarding the hiring of individual teachers
10. Decisions as to which of various factors are used in determining individual grades (such as exam scores, attendance, behavior).

To measure perceptions of influence, each respondent (whether student, SG member, teacher, or principal) was asked to rate the influence of each potential influential, in each of the 10 decision areas, on a four-point scale: 1, no influence; 2, a little influence; 3, moderate influence; 4, a lot of influence (plus 0 for "don't know").

Degree of Ignorance about Influence

Before we consider the responses to these influence questions, it is important to examine the proportion of the several respondent groups who answered "don't know." If the frequency of "don't know" responses is high, either overall or for particular classes of influentials or decision types, then we may conclude that the perceived influence structure is opaque – that it is hard for people involved to determine who has influence – and that the responses do not necessarily present an accurate picture of actual influence.

In table 1, the "don't know" responses are tabulated by decision area (averaging over potential influentials) and in table 2 they are tabulated by type of in-

Table 1/Percentages of Students, Student Government Members, and Teachers Who "Don't Know" How Much Influence Is Exerted on Various School Decision Areas, Averaged Across Influentials

Decision Area	Students	SG Members	Teachers[a]
School rules re appearance	8.8	6.9	5.3
School rules re smoking	8.6	7.6	5.1
Other school rules	9.6	8.8	6.0
School rules re political activities	12.1	10.5	7.4
Introduction of new courses	6.4	5.6	3.0
Courses students take	6.7	6.5	3.2
Disciplining students	7.9	6.5	3.6
Evaluation of teachers	11.4	9.6	4.5
Hiring of individual teachers	9.3	8.0	3.0
Grading students	8.0	7.0	3.5

a. Teacher data do not include the last two respondent groups: "your close friends" and "you yourself." These were designed only for students and SG members.

Table 2/Percentages of Students, Student Government Members, and Teachers Who "Don't Know" How Much Influence Is Exerted by Various Potential Influentials, Averaged Across 10 School Decision Areas

Potential Influentials	Students	SG Members	Teachers[a]
Ontario Ministry of Education	22.2	23.1	10.4
Board of education, director of education, or superintendent	16.0	14.7	5.4
Principals or vice-principals	5.0	4.0	1.3
Teachers	5.7	4.4	1.5
SG members	5.9	3.6	4.9
Students in general	4.8	3.3	3.3
Close friends	6.0	4.3	
Yourself	5.3	4.0	

a. Teacher data do not include the last two respondent groups: "your close friends" and "you yourself." These were designed only for students and SG members.

fluential (averaging across decision areas). In both cases, principals' responses are excluded because very few answered "don't know."

We first note that "don't know" response rates are generally low. As one would expect, however, the rates are highest among students and lowest among teachers, with SG members in between. Across decision areas (table 1), the expressed ignorance rates are quite similar, the highest being only 12.1% for student judgments regarding political activity rules.[6]

Turning to table 2, we note that ignorance rates among students and SG members and, to a lesser degree, teachers are particularly high for the two potential influentials outside the school, the board of education and the Ministry of Education. The figures are highest for the Ministry, which is furthest removed from the school. For the rest of the potential influentials, the "don't know" rates are similar, except that teachers profess almost as much ignorance about the influence of student government as about that of the board of education. Again, what is most striking about all of these figures is that, with the exceptions that have been noted, the rates are quite low. While not all estimations of influence may be completely accurate, the vast majority of respondents appear to believe that they know enough to make estimations.

How Much Influence Do Student Governments Have?

Table 3 presents the perceptions of the four opinion groups regarding SG influence in each of the 10 decision areas. The decisions are listed in order of the principals' perceptions – the first decision area (political activity rules) being the one over which principals see student governments exerting the most influence and the last (hiring of teachers) being the one over which principals see student governments exerting the least influence. All the opinion groups agree that these are the highest and lowest areas, respectively, of SG influence. Furthermore, with a few minor exceptions, the other opinion groups tend to agree with the principals' rank ordering of the rest of the decisions (that is, all four groups perceive SG influence as higher for other school rules, appearance regulations, and smoking rules, and lower for rules governing the courses students take, teacher evaluation, and student grading).

Table 3/Average Principal, Student, Student Government Member, and Teacher Ratings of Student Government Influence in Various School Decision Areas

Decision Area[a]	*Principals*	*Students*	*SG Members*	*Teachers*
School rules re political activities	3.2	2.2	2.7	2.8
Other school rules	2.8	2.3	2.1	2.1
School rules re appearance	2.7	2.0	1.9	2.2
School rules re smoking	2.6	2.2	2.1	2.2
Disciplining students	2.2	1.9	1.9	1.7
Introduction of new courses	2.1	2.1	1.9	1.6
Courses student take	1.7	1.7	1.5	1.4
Evaluation of teachers	1.6	1.9	1.6	1.4
Grading students	1.6	1.6	1.4	1.3
Hiring of individual teachers	1.2	1.3	1.1	1.0

Note: 1, no influence; 2, a little influence; 3, moderate influence; 4, a lot of influence.
a. Ranked in order of the principals' perceptions.

While all opinion groups agree generally on the rank ordering of the decision areas, in some cases there is substantial disagreement about the *absolute* level of influence student governments have over various decisions. For example, while the average rating by principals of SG influence over political activity rules is 3.2 (slightly more than moderate influence), the students' average rating of SG influence in this area is a full point lower, indicating slightly more than a little influence. Looking at this another way, while 40.6% of the principals rate student governments as having a great deal of influence over political activity rules, only 23% of SG members and a mere 8% of teachers share this opinion.

It is instructive to relate these ratings to the subjects of frequent student protest activity discussed in Chapter 1. Although student governments are considered to have their greatest influence over political activity rules, one of the major concerns of the rapidly developing students' bill of rights movement is the governance of political activities by students (note the calls for freedom of the press, freedom of speech, and freedom of assembly, which are central to the various proposed bill of rights). Similarly, although student governments are rated as having relatively high influence over rules governing appearance and smoking, these are also some of the issues over which students have protested most often.

At first glance this situation may seem contradictory, since one might expect that students would be least likely to protest in areas where they feel influence can be exerted through formal and legitimate channels (that is, through the student government). One partial explanation of this apparent anomaly may be found in the ratings of *absolute* level of influence. Although students (and SG members) agree that SG influence is relatively higher in these areas, in no case do these groups, on the average, assign as much as moderate influence (an average influence score of 3) to student governments, and in almost all cases the average influence rating is near 2 (a little influence). Thus, what may be most frustrating to students who desire change is that even in those areas where student governments are seen to have the greatest influence, the absolute level is seen to be low.

Of all of these decision areas, smoking rules have been the most contentious issue during the past few years (seeming to replace the issue of hair length, which excited popular opinion during the late 1960s). As a recent example, in March 1974, the Toronto Board of Education decided to open the possibility for student smoking lounges to be established in secondary schools under its jurisdiction. This was undoubtedly gratifying to many students, as the single most common complaint we have heard (especially from older students) in interviews and comments submitted with our questionnaires is the lack of a smoking area in their school. But the editorial pages of Toronto newspapers were immediately filled with letters complaining that the schools were abdicating their responsibility to teach students the dangers of smoking. The board subsequently reversed its decision and imposed more severe smoking restrictions than had previously existed.

This issue highlights the various pressures that act to produce change in the schools and demonstrates how influence may be exerted by students in ways that are not immediately apparent to the observer or even to the students themselves. About one-fourth of the principals in our survey claimed that the student government in their school had a great deal of influence over smoking rules. Only 10% of the SG members and 11% of the teachers agreed, and nearly one-third of the student body felt their student government had no influence whatsoever over smoking rules.

In a different section of the questionnaire, we asked students if there had been any changes in smoking rules since they had been in their current secondary school. About 40% of the students claimed that there had been such changes since they had been in their school. In only three schools (7.9% of our sample) did more than 80% of the students acknowledge that a rule change in smoking had occurred since they had been there. In four schools, 65% to 80% of the students identified a change since they had been in school. Ten percent or more of the students in 86.9% of the schools we surveyed said a change in smoking rules had occurred. Presumably (but we have not been able to verify this), the lower the percentage, the older the change. If this is the case, then in the nine schools where only 20% to 34% of the students say a change occurred, the students are probably in grades 12 and 13 and the change probably occurred during their first year in school.

The puzzle here is this: student governments are not perceived by the students as being strongly influential in effecting changes in smoking rules; yet, in a vast majority of schools, a substantial percentage of students testifies that during their attendance the smoking rules have been changed and principals rate student governments as more influential in this area than do students. It may be assumed that in most instances the changes reduced rather than increased restrictions on smoking. It is, of course, possible that principals voluntarily reduced restrictions or that they responded to pressures from sources outside their school, and students failed to associate these pressures with students or student governments in other schools.

One school we visited had recently changed its smoking rules from prohibiting students to smoke anywhere on the school grounds to providing a location, within the school, for students to smoke. The vice-principal reported that this decision was made because at the end of each day he would have a line of students outside his office who had been caught smoking in the washroom. Neither the principal nor the vice-principal could work out a technique to stop the consistent violation of the smoking rules, and they decided that their inability to enforce no-smoking regulations, coupled with the risk of fire, warranted a more open policy. The vice-principal indicated that he was happy with the change, in large part because it greatly reduced the number of students he had to see about breaking the rule. In this case, the students seemed to be influential in bringing about the change through an unplanned program of rule violation.

It is our impression from interviews that this may be a common pattern. Student governments often keep the issue of smoking privileges alive by promising to do all in their power to get the administration to provide an appropriate smoking lounge. However, when regulations have been relaxed the principal has been responding to the "pressure of public opinion" in his school (to which any good administrator must be attuned in some way). Although the student government may have been the vehicle for verbalizing the issue, and keeping it before the principal, the lack of any dramatic confrontations over the question of smoking privileges has obscured from students, and the SG members themselves, the role their constant pressure has played in stimulating the change. If this is indeed a pattern that occurs in many schools across many decision areas, it could account for the fact that principals generally ascribe more influence to student governments than do students themselves.

How Much Influence Do Students Have?

We now consider the degree of influence perceived to be exerted by students, rather than student governments. Table 4 presents the average influence rating assigned to students in their own school by each of the four respondent groups. As in table 3, the decisions are ranked in order of the principals' perception of student influence.

In interpreting these ratings, a word of caution is necessary. In some decision areas, different people interpreted the questions in different ways. For example, with regard to the question concerning rules about appearance, we were thinking of restrictive rules (that is, rules that constrain choices), such as "students may not wear blue jeans," "girls may not wear miniskirts," "male students must wear jackets and ties to assemblies," or "males must be clean shaven." We were interested in finding out who influences changes in these rules. We were therefore surprised to find that all of the opinion groups believed that students influenced appearance rules more than student governments did. It is true that there have been many instances when members of the student body have effectively petitioned or engaged in some kind of protest in order to get a rule change, and some of the respondents may have been thinking of the changes that occurred as a result of such activities. In other cases, however, respondents were probably

Table 4/Average Principal, Student, Student Government Member, and Teacher Ratings of Student Influence in Various School Decision Areas

Decision Area[a]	Principals	Students	SG Members	Teachers
Courses students take	3.6	2.5	2.4	3.0
School rules re appearance	3.4	2.5	2.4	3.2
School rules re political activities	2.6	2.2	2.2	1.9
Introduction of new courses	2.6	2.2	2.1	1.9
School rules re smoking	2.6	2.2	2.0	2.3
Other school rules	2.5	2.0	1.8	2.0
Evaluation of teachers	2.2	2.1	1.9	1.8
Disciplining students	2.1	1.8	1.7	1.7
Grading students	1.9	1.6	1.4	1.4
Hiring of individual teachers	1.1	1.3	1.2	1.1

Note: 1, no influence; 2, a little influence; 3, moderate influence; 4, a lot of influence.
a. Ranked in order of the principals' perceptions.

thinking not so much of rule changes as of the students' ability to exercise personal choice in attire – choice that resulted from changes in, or the elimination of, restrictive rules.

In other cases, the principal and the student government may tap student opinion in a number of areas. One principal stated that he and his student government "issued questionnaires to students regarding courses for next year, extra-curricular activities, dress regulations . . . and various school policies." Because this school provides a mechanism whereby students can register their concerns, the principal may ascribe more influence to students than to the student government. In most decision areas, this kind of ambiguity is not a problem. Where it is a problem, it is probable that differences in interpretation are distributed equally among various opinion groups.

Principals believe that students have their greatest influence over the courses they actually take. This view is hardly surprising, since with the introduction of the credit system the provincial government has mandated greater student choice in this area. However, what is noteworthy is that although course choice is seen by students and SG members as one of the decision areas over which they have greatest influence (in both cases tied with appearance rules for first place), the absolute level of influence over course choice that students ascribe to themselves (2.5) is more than a full point lower, on a four-point scale, than the absolute level ascribed to them by principals (3.6). It appears that, whatever the wishes of the provincial Ministry of Education, and whatever principals believe to be happening, students see their actual choice of courses as being much more constrained by other decision-makers than do principals.

Among the other decision areas, principals believe that students have their greatest influence over appearance rules: 58.3% ($N=21$) of the principals said the students had a great deal in influence and not one said they had no influence. Only 29% of the students believed they had a great deal of influence, and an equal percentage believed they had no influence whatsoever. The SG members responded much the same way as did the students. The teachers' perceptions, however, were more like the principals': 51% believed that students had a great deal of influence over appearance rules, while 9.3% ($N=137$) saw students in their schools as having no influence whatsoever.

The data in table 5 can be summarized by four points:
1. All groups agree that, in the 10 decision areas, students have their greatest influence over the courses they take[7] and over rules concerning student appearance. Principals see the students as being more influential than the students believe themselves to be.
2. There is general agreement that students have a little to moderate influence over all other areas save one, namely, the hiring of teachers. All opinion groups recognize that student influence in this domain is minimal.
3. On our scale, ranging from 1 to 4, the number 2.5 represents a midpoint. A rating greater than 2.5 can be viewed as a swing toward higher influence, and a lesser rating as a swing toward low influence. Principals classify students as swinging toward the high influence end of the scale in six decisions, teachers in two, students in two, and SG members in one.

Table 5/Views of Principals, Students, Student Government Members, and Teachers on Desired Increases or Decreases in Student Influence in Various School Decision Areas

Decision Area[a]	Principals	Students	SG Members	Teachers
Grading students	.4	.8	1.0	.5
Disciplining students	.1	.5	.6	.4
School rules re smoking	.1	.7	.9	.1
Introduction of new courses	0	.8	.8	.6
Hiring of individual teachers	0	.4	.4	.2
School rules re appearance	−.1	.8	1.1	−.2
Other school rules	−.1	.5	.9	.3
Evaluation of teachers	−.1	.2	.4	0
Courses students take	−.4	.7	.9	−.1
School rules re political activities	−.4	.3	.5	.4

Note: Read in conjunction with tables 3 and 4.
a. Ranked in order of principals' perceptions.

4. When teachers' ratings of student influence are compared to their ratings of SG influence, it appears that teachers believe students are more influential than are student governments. In only two areas do teachers rate SG influence higher than student influence (rules concerning political activities and other school rules) and in one area (disciplining students) teachers regard both groups as equally influential. This view is not completely shared by principals. They rate student governments as being more influential than are students in four areas (rules concerning political activities, other school rules, disciplining students, and hiring teachers) and regard the two groups as equally influential in one area (smoking rules).

How Much Influence Ought Students To Have?

To determine the level of influence that each opinion group believes students ought to have, we estimated the changes – that is, increases or decreases in influence – that would take place if each opinion group's ideas were implemented (see table 5). It is useful to read table 5 in conjunction with tables 3 and 4 to get an idea of the point from which each group wishes changes to occur.

In general, the principals support the status quo, in most cases desiring either modest or no changes. They do, however, wish significant changes in three areas. They would like to see a substantial decrease in student influence over decisions regarding political activities and courses students take;[8] and they would like an increase in student influence over grading procedures. It is interesting to note that of the eight areas where principals wish some change, they desire *decreases* of influence in five.

The views of students and SG members are generally consistent. Both groups

43

want major *increases* in influence over school rules regarding appearance, school rules regarding smoking, introduction of new courses, courses students take, and grading students.

SG members are more eager than is the student body to increase student control over "other school rules."

In most decision areas, teachers would like students to have greater influence than they currently enjoy. Specifically, they would like some increase in students' influence over the introduction of new courses and in students' power to deal with disciplinary problems. They also support the principals in their wish to increase student influence over factors in student grades but disagree with the principals' desire to reduce SG control over political activity rules. Rather, they would increase student control in this area. Teachers do, however, support the principals in their belief that students have too much influence over appearance rules and course choices, and say they would like to see small reductions in student influence in these areas.

In summary, we have observed significant areas of agreement and disagreement among the four opinion groups. We assume that in areas where all groups agree that student influence should be increased, it will be generally easier to achieve such an increase (although this will vary from school to school). Where students and SG members desire an increase in student influence – in effect, in all 10 decision areas – and teachers or principals desire a decrease, more conflict can be expected and there is a lesser probability of achieving real increases in student influence.

The area where all opinion groups agree that student influence should be increased is grading. For principals, this is the area where the greatest increase is desired. Among teachers and students, it ranks second in priority for increased influence. Among SG members, this decision area is ranked with two others for greatest desired influence increase.

Another area of (more modest) agreement is student discipline. Students, SG members, and teachers all desire roughly the same degree of increase in student influence over discipline, while principals on the average wish at least a small increase.

There is also agreement regarding increase of student influence over smoking rules. Students and SG members want a substantial increase, and teachers and principals are prepared to grant at least some increase.

The introduction of new courses is another area where there is some agreement. Students, SG members, and teachers all wish fairly substantial increases in student influence; principals, however, wish no increase. It should be noted that in this area principals ascribed more current influence to students than did any of the three other groups (see table 4).

Finally, there is at least modest agreement regarding the desirability of increasing student influence over the hiring of teachers. No group sees students as having much current influence in this area. Students, SG members, and teachers desire very modest influence increases, while principals again wish no change.

It is encouraging, from a pedagogical point of view, that of the five areas where the probability for relatively conflict-free increases in student influence is fairly high, three refer to the substance of schooling – grading students, the introduction of new courses, and hiring of individual teachers. The other two areas – smoking rules and student discipline – refer to the regulation of student conduct.

The remaining five decision areas represent more substantial inter-group disagreements, with consequent lower probabilities of achieving conflict-free increases in student influence. In two areas, other school rules and political activity rules, all groups except principals desire at least modest increases in student influence; here principals desire a *decrease* (in the latter area, one of the two largest decreases desired by principals). In the area of teacher evaluation, students and SG members desire small increases in influence, teachers desire no change, and principals desire a very small decrease.

In two areas, there is a clear division of opinion between students and staff – appearance rules and the courses students take. In both cases, students and SG members desire sizable increases in influence, while both teachers and principals desire modest decreases in student influence. It should be noted, however, that in both areas the *absolute* ideal level of student influence differs little across groups. In the appearance area, the average influence level desired by principals and students is 3.3; by SG members, 3.5; and by teachers, 3.0. Regarding courses taken by students, the average level desired by both students and principals is 3.2; by SG members, 3.3; and by teachers, 2.9. In both cases, the direction of change desired relates to perception of the current situation. Principals and teachers perceive students as having greater influence than do the two groups of students themselves. Thus, principals and teachers see a decrease as necessary to reach the desired end state, while students and SG members would require an increase to reach the same desired level.

How Should Students Participate in Decision-making?

After viewing the levels of influence desired by students and SG members, one might well get the impression that both groups are eager and willing to take over decision-making in a number of areas. But, as previously suggested, asking someone how much influence they desire is a somewhat vague and ambiguous question. We therefore asked the four opinion groups what they believe to be the most desirable *procedure* by which students should exercise the desired influence. Did they believe that they should have complete authority over the decision area, should they share this authority by participating directly with the principal and other staff members, should they simply offer their opinions to the principal and staff, or should they exclude themselves altogether? The responses are presented in table 6.

Although SG members desire the greatest increases in influence, there is not a single decision area where a majority wants total control. They indicate that they want the greatest increase in influence over appearance rules, yet only 25% of them believe that students should have complete control of this area. In the case of students deciding what courses they want, 49% recommend complete student control but nearly 30% believe that students should simply give their ideas to the staff, who would then make the final decision.

Table 6/Views of Principals, Students, Student Government Members, and Teachers on the Best Way for Students to Participate in Decision-Making in Various School Decision Areas

Decision Area	1. Students should have complete control N	%	2. Students and staff should both vote N	%	3. Students should give their ideas to staff and staff decide N	%	4. Students should have little or no say N	%	Total N	Influence through Authority (Score of 1 & 2) N	%
School rules re appearance											
Principals	6	17.1	11	31.4	18	51.4	0	—	35	17	48.5
Students	699	24.7	1101	38.9	1002	36.4	129	1.0	2831	1800	63.6
SG members	210	25.1	334	39.9	285	34.1	8	.9	837	544	65.0
Teachers	94	6.3	456	30.4	891	59.4	58	3.9	1499	550	36.7
School rules re smoking											
Principals	1	2.8	3	8.3	28	77.8	4	11.1	36	4	11.1
Students	270	9.5	1202	42.4	1176	41.5	185	6.6	2833	1472	51.9
SG members	61	7.3	359	42.9	377	45.0	40	4.8	837	420	50.2
Teachers	20	1.3	301	19.9	983	65.0	208	13.8	1512	321	21.2
Other school rules											
Principals	1	2.8	2	5.6	31	86.1	2	5.6	36	3	8.4
Students	270	9.5	1132	39.9	1227	43.3	206	7.3	2838	1402	49.4
SG members	53	6.4	340	40.9	395	47.4	44	5.3	832	393	47.3
Teachers	22	1.5	279	18.4	1030	68.0	183	12.1	1514	301	19.9
School rules re political activities											
Principals	1	2.9	4	11.4	28	80.0	2	5.7	35	5	14.3
Students	334	11.8	1015	35.8	1271	44.8	218	7.6	2838	1349	47.6
SG members	102	12.2	335	40.2	354	42.5	42	5.1	833	437	52.4
Teachers	29	1.9	333	22.0	991	65.5	161	10.6	1514	362	23.9

Introduction of											
new courses											
Principals	0	–	5	14.3	29	82.9	1	2.9	35	5	14.3
Students	188	6.6	878	30.8	1588	55.8	190	6.8	2844	1066	37.4
SG members	42	5.0	246	29.3	497	59.2	55	6.2	840	288	34.3
Teachers	6	.4	165	10.9	1206	79.8	135	8.9	1512	171	11.3
Courses students take											
Principals	12	35.3	7	20.6	14	41.2	1	2.9	34	19	55.9
Students	1414	50.0	499	17.6	798	28.2	116	4.1	2827	1913	67.6
SG members	400	49.2	139	17.1	241	29.6	33	4.1	813	539	66.3
Teachers	295	20.3	276	19.0	793	54.6	88	6.1	1452	571	39.3
Disciplining students											
Principals	0	–	2	5.6	24	66.7	10	27.8	36	2	5.6
Students	187	6.6	886	31.2	1318	46.4	449	15.8	2840	1073	37.8
SG members	41	4.9	273	32.7	405	48.5	116	13.9	835	314	37.6
Teachers	23	1.5	235	15.7	889	59.3	353	23.5	1500	258	17.2
Evaluation											
of teachers											
Principals	0	–	0	–	23	66.6	11	32.4	34	0	–
Students	375	13.3	738	26.1	1255	44.4	458	16.2	2826	1113	39.4
SG members	92	11.0	222	26.6	382	45.7	139	16.7	835	314	37.6
Teachers	41	2.8	219	14.8	663	44.7	516	37.8	1484	260	17.6
Hiring of											
individual teachers											
Principals	0	–	1	2.8	4	11.1	31	86.1	36	1	2.8
Students	61	2.2	348	12.3	875	30.8	1552	54.7	2836	409	14.5
SG members	7	.8	93	11.1	253	30.1	488	58.0	841	100	11.9
Teachers	5	.3	38	2.5	224	14.9	1237	82.2	1504	43	2.8
Grading students											
Principals	0	–	4	11.1	27	75.0	5	13.9	36	4	11.1
Students	141	4.9	804	28.4	1358	48.0	526	18.6	2829	945	33.3
SG members	24	2.9	248	29.7	422	50.5	142	16.9	836	272	32.6
Teachers	5	.3	145	9.7	847	56.4	505	33.6	1502	150	10.0

Principals believe that student governments exert their greatest influence over rules concerning political activities and that such influence should be reduced. SG members want to increase their influence in this area, yet only 12% of them believe students should have complete control over political activity rules and an additional 41% believe that students and staff should decide jointly. Fully 48% want to participate indirectly, by communicating their ideas to staff and the principal.

It should be noted that we are distinguishing between two types of influence. The first is influence in decision-making through authority. This is the case where an individual or individuals have been delegated the formal authority with which to exercise decision-making power. This authority can be used alone, as when one constituency or individual monopolizes power, or it can be shared. The second form of influence in decision-making is through communication. Here the individual or group has no formal authority but has access to formal or informal lines of communication with the formal decision-maker(s). The percentages of each group who think students should have influence through authority in the 10 decision areas are presented in the last column of table 6.

In only four of the decision areas do a majority of SG members favor participation through authority. Of these four, there are but two – political activity rules and smoking rules – over which student governments may be expected to exert a great deal of influence. In the other two areas, appearance rules and course selection, individual student choices seem more important. Issues that have been raised among students in some jurisdictions deal with general school rules, the introduction of new courses, student discipline, teacher evaluation, hiring of teachers, and factors affecting students' grades. Yet in none of these areas does a majority of SG members desire direct participation. In fact, in all six of these areas, more SG members believe that students should have little or no say than think they should have complete control. Student views closely parallel those of SG members.

In looking at the principals' views of how participation should take place, it seems clear that they are not inclined toward granting authority to students. Indirect participation, through communication, is preferred by a majority of principals in eight of 10 decision areas.

In the ninth case – the hiring of teachers – principals are almost unanimous in wanting to exclude students altogether from the decision-making process. (In this area, however, the vast majority of students wants either no influence or influence through communication.) In only one case does a majority of principals (56%) favor students having complete control. This, of course, is over course choices.

There are five areas where a greater percentage of teachers than principals favors student participation in decision-making through authority. This is partly a function of the level of influence that each opinion group believes students and student governments already possess. Still, proportionally more teachers than principals favor student participation through authority in appearance rules, smoking rules, political activities, other school rules, disciplinary regulations, and, interestingly, teacher evaluation. A smaller percentage of teachers than of principals would like student participation by authority in appearance rules and the courses that students take. In no area do more than 40% of the teachers favor student participation by authority, and in eight of 10 decision areas less than 25% of the teachers favor student participation through shared authority.

In sum, then, in only two areas do a substantial number of students or SG members desire complete control – appearance rules and the courses they take. Even in the latter case, only 50% of students want such control. In only three areas – the above two plus smoking rules – do a majority of students and SG members desire influence through authority. But although student aspirations are relatively modest, in every case a smaller percentage (in all but two cases, *substantially* smaller) of teachers and principals wishes students to exert influence through authority. There are only three areas where the *modal* response for each group is not the same – the now familiar areas of appearance rules, smoking rules, and course choice.

How Dissatisfied Are Students with School Rules and Policies?

We next consider the extent to which the desire for higher levels of influence among students and SG members reflects a strong sense of dissatisfaction with the rules or policies and procedures their schools now have in force in the various decision areas. We asked students and SG members to tell us whether they thought the rules and procedures and policies in their school in a number of areas were very bad, bad, moderate (neither good nor bad), good, or very good. The responses of both groups are presented in table 7. As another measure of dissatisfaction, we asked students and SG members to indicate which one of the same list of rules and procedures and policies they thought most needed changing in their school. The responses are presented in table 8.

Before these responses are compared to the desired levels of influence increase, a general comment is in order. These students do not seem to be very dissatisfied. Looking at table 7, we see that in no case do more than 27% of either group regard anything on the list as bad or very bad. In only one case, the way students are disciplined, do fewer than one-third of the two groups think that current practices are good or very good. Looking at modal responses, we find that in all 22 cases (11 areas × 2 respondent groups) the modal response is either moderate (12 cases) or good (10 cases). In all cases, the vast majority of respondents feel the situation is good, or at least adequate, in their schools. Thus, when we speak of differing levels of dissatisfaction, we are speaking of differences starting from a very small base. This impression is reinforced by table 8. When forced to choose one area as most needing change, the respondents come to no consensus. Seventeen percent of students claim nothing needs to be changed. In the specifically mentioned areas, in no case do more than 12% of either group agree that a particular item most needs alteration.

We compare these responses with the desire for increased influence among SG members, since they are the official representatives of students in general and presumably have some feel for the desires of their constituents. Moreover, this comparison provides useful background for our more detailed consideration of student governments in later chapters.

Table 7/Opinions of Students and Student Government Members on Various School Rules and Policies

Rules and Policies	Very Bad N	Very Bad %	Bad N	Bad %	Moderate N	Moderate %	Good N	Good %	Very Good N	Very Good %	Total N	Total %
Students												
School rules re appearance	67	2.4	132	4.7	606	21.4	1128	39.8	900	31.8	2833	100.1
School rules re smoking	244	8.7	361	12.8	931	33.0	916	32.5	368	13.0	2820	100.0
Other school rules	175	6.2	369	13.1	1032	36.7	898	31.9	341	12.1	2815	100.0
School rules re political activities	104	3.7	247	8.9	1190	42.7	949	34.0	299	10.7	2789	100.0
Way courses are taught	89	3.1	226	8.0	1304	46.0	1036	36.5	182	6.4	2837	100.0
Types of courses given	64	2.3	165	5.8	946	33.4	1217	42.9	444	15.6	2836	100.0
Cafeteria policies	263	9.7	363	13.3	785	28.8	910	33.4	400	14.7	2721	99.9
Assignment to courses	56	2.0	169	6.0	749	26.6	1187	42.2	654	23.2	2815	100.0
Disciplining students	154	5.5	370	13.2	1369	48.8	767	27.3	145	5.2	2805	100.0
Grading students	135	4.9	357	12.9	1324	47.8	821	29.7	130	4.7	2767	100.0
Kinds of social activities	255	9.3	366	13.4	867	31.7	827	30.3	416	15.2	2731	99.9
Student Government Members												
School rules re appearance	17	2.0	24	2.9	156	18.6	339	40.5	302	36.0	838	100.0
School rules re smoking	60	7.1	120	14.3	257	30.6	302	35.9	111	13.2	840	100.1
Other school rules	35	4.2	116	13.8	293	35.0	275	32.8	117	14.0	838	99.8
School rules re political activities	29	3.5	77	9.3	346	41.6	286	34.5	92	11.1	829	100.0
Way courses are taught	24	2.9	83	9.9	398	47.6	279	33.3	53	6.3	837	100.0
Types of courses given	8	1.0	48	5.7	281	33.4	367	43.7	136	16.2	840	100.0
Cafeteria policies	100	12.5	110	13.7	214	26.7	258	32.2	120	15.0	802	100.1
Assignment to courses	16	1.9	43	5.1	194	23.2	380	45.5	203	24.3	836	100.0
Disciplining students	41	4.9	99	11.9	413	49.5	238	28.5	43	5.2	834	100.0
Grading students	45	5.5	101	12.4	390	47.7	248	30.4	33	4.0	817	100.0
Kinds of social activities	58	7.1	94	11.5	251	30.8	268	32.8	145	17.8	816	100.0

Table 8/Views of Students and Student Government Members on What Most Needs Changing in Their School

Area of Change	Students Total	%	SG Members Total	%
Nothing needs to be changed	441	17.0	77	10.2
School rules re smoking	290	11.2	71	9.5
Grading students	263	10.2	77	10.2
Kinds of social activities	247	9.5	78	10.3
Way courses are taught	215	8.3	87	11.5
Disciplining students	190	7.3	58	7.6
Cafeteria services	179	6.9	58	7.6
Other school rules	145	5.6	39	5.1
Types of courses offered	116	4.5	32	4.2
School rules re appearance	104	4.0	19	2.5
Assignment to courses	80	3.1	23	3.0
School rules re political activities	68	2.6	18	2.4
Other	253	9.8	121	16.0
Total	2591	100.0	758	100.0

In table 9, the decision areas are ordered by degree of influence increase desired by SG members (lefthand column). Next to each decision area is indicated the percentage of students who feel that the situation in their school in each area is bad or very bad. (The correspondence between the rows is not in all cases exact – see footnotes c and d.) SG members do not generally wish increases in level of influence in relation to the degree of dissatisfaction indicated by students. They desire the greatest influence increase in precisely the area, appearance rules, where students are *least* dissatisfied. It would, however, be a mistake to conclude that, in general, increases in students' desires for influence in an area are inversely related to their satisfaction in that area. Actually, there is neither a positive nor a negative relationship: the two factors are independent.

It may be encouraging to note that the three areas mentioned earlier where increases in student influence were most likely to be achieved without conflict – grading students, disciplining of students, and smoking rules – are, respectively, the fourth and third highest and the highest areas of student dissatisfaction.

In any case, the data in table 9 suggest that SG members may not be very well attuned to what their student constituents most want. Our impression from these and other survey data, plus the case studies, is that student governments neither possess nor desire a great deal of autonomy over the creation or alteration of rules, regulations, or policies affecting school life. It seems that few student governments have ever represented the students in a bargaining mode or in

Table 9/Correspondence Between Student Government Members' Degree of Desire for Increased Student Influence and Students' Levels of Dissatisfaction in Various School Decision Areas

Area of Desired Influence Increase[a]	SG Members' Degree of Desired Influence Increase	% of Students Dissatisfied[b]
School rules re appearance	1.1	7.1
Grading students	1.0	17.8
School rules re smoking	.9	21.5
Other school rules	.9	19.3
Courses students take	.9	8.0
Introduction of new courses	.8	8.1[c]
Disciplining students	.6	18.7
School rules re political activities	.5	12.6
Evaluation of teachers	.4	11.1[d]
Hiring of individual teachers	.4	

$\gamma = -.06$ (γ is a statistical measure of the strength of the association between the two rank orderings. A γ of $-.06$ indicates that the two rank orderings are essentially unrelated – that there is no relationship between them.)
a. Ranked in order of degree of desired increase.
b. Students who rated the present situation as "bad" or "very bad."
c. Question refers to "types of courses offered."
d. Question refers to "way courses are taught."

matters requiring conflict resolution. Their actual and desired influence has given them little sensitivity to or experience in the political process and has probably done little toward helping them develop broad sets of decision-making and analytical skills – even such elementary ones as keeping in tune with the wishes of their constituents.

Along the same lines, we note that one of the most basic elements in the decision-making process is knowing where or knowing how to find out where the appropriate location of authority lies for specific decisions. In one of the case studies we conducted, students had been pressuring their student government over the past several years to get them a smoking area within the school. We spoke to students who were SG members and asked them the reason for the absence of a smoking area. Some told us that fire regulations prohibited smoking in all areas outside the staff smoking room; others told us that it was a board policy not to let students smoke in the building; and some said that the Ministry of Education had passed a rule prohibiting smoking. Not one SG member had bothered calling the board, the fire department, or the Ministry in an effort to secure information concerning their smoking policies with respect to the school. Yet nearly all these students had promised a smoking area for students while giving their campaign speeches in the school assembly.

Does this sound like rather poor scholarship on the part of these students? Seventy-five percent of the principals believe that the Ministry of Education has no influence whatsoever on smoking policies, but only 34% of SG members believe the Ministry has no influence and nearly 30% think the Ministry has a great deal of influence over smoking policies (see table 10). It seems that the most likely area for increased student participation is over factors influencing student grades. Less than 3% of the principals in the survey think the Ministry has a great deal of influence over this area, but 35% of SG members believe the Ministry has a great deal of influence over factors influencing student grades.

Indeed, we find that in all decision areas except the courses students actually take, students and SG members ascribe more influence to the Ministry of Education than do principals. Assuming that principals have a better fix on the "real" influence of the Ministry, and combining this survey data with the case study example just given, we conclude that SG members in general neither know nor know how to find out very much about the influences that are operating upon their schools. They may be able to map fairly accurately the patterns of influence within their school, among the individuals they see every day or week, but they seem unable to decode the wider environment that affects their school.

To summarize, it is useful to break down the 10 decision areas into two categories: non-academic decisions and academic decisions. There are five areas that may be considered non-academic decisions: rules about appearance, smoking, political activities, discipline, and other school rules. The remaining five pertain to academic decisions: rules about the introduction of new courses, the courses students take, evaluation of teachers, the hiring of teachers, and factors used in determining individual grades.

Non-Academic Decisions

In the non-academic area, there are no decisions over which students or SG members desire complete control. A majority or near-majority would prefer influence through shared authority. In most decisions, however, a large minority of students and SG members oppose delegating authority to student representatives. Rather, they would have their representatives provide information on student opinions and propose solutions, but retain the formal decision-making authority in the hands of the principal and his staff. Only in appearance rules does a clear majority of students and SG members favor direct student participation in the decision-making process. Presumably, there are not many issues to resolve in this area as three-quarters of the students report that they are quite satisfied with the appearance rules in their school.

Perhaps principals, too, recognize the "safety" of direct student participation in decisions concerning appearance rules, for this is the area in which most principals are willing to permit students to share formal authority. In other non-academic decisions, however, principals and teachers agree that students should exercise their influence by communication and persuasion only.

While a greater percentage of students than principals desires student influence in non-academic decisions through authority, it cannot be claimed that students are of a single voice. In general, they are evenly divided: although virtually all believe that student representatives should have a say in decision-making, half believes that say should be through the sharing of formal authority

Table 10/Views of Student Government Members, Students, and Principals on the Ministry of Education's Influence in Various School Decision Areas

	Degree of Ministry Influence Perceived (%)						Average Rating[a]		
	A Lot			None					
Decision Area	SG Members	Students	Principals	SG Members	Students	Principals	SG Members	Students	Principals
School rules re appearance	14.1	16.4	5.7	43.4	35.6	68.6	2.0	2.2	1.5
School rules re smoking	28.7	32.4	5.9	34.0	29.6	76.5	2.4	2.6	1.4
Other school rules	9.2	12.9	5.9	60.3	50.0	76.5	1.7	1.9	1.3
School rules re political activities	18.7	24.8	6.1	37.5	29.2	57.6	2.2	2.4	1.6
Introduction of new courses	70.5	70.5	38.9	3.9	4.8	5.6	3.6	3.5	3.1
Courses students take	23.7	22.0	28.6	46.0	43.0	14.3	2.1	1.3	2.7
Disciplining students	17.3	21.2	8.6	35.3	31.1	34.3	2.2	2.3	2.1
Evaluation of teachers	46.0	48.9	5.7	14.7	12.0	42.9	3.0	3.1	1.7
Hiring of individual teachers	41.9	49.8	9.1	19.2	12.9	36.7	2.8	3.1	2.0
Grading students	35.0	38.6	2.8	18.8	17.7	38.9	2.8	2.8	1.8

a. 1, no influence; 2, a little influence; 3, moderate influence; 4, a lot of influence.

and the other half believes that student representatives should confine themselves to a communication role.

Academic Decisions

In general, neither students nor principals believe that student governments possess much influence in academic decisions. Furthermore, neither students nor principals would like to see authority delegated to student representatives in these areas. With the exception of the hiring of teachers, all opinion groups opt for students communicating any ideas they might have to the decision-makers, who will then make the final decision. All groups believe that students have no legitimate role in deciding on the hiring of teachers.

The split among secondary school students over whether or not they prefer a strong and direct voice in decisions affecting them helps explain why principals who are philosophically in favor of student participation write such comments as the following:

A major problem is how to make student councils operate effectively without leading them by the hand. If they operate by themselves, they inevitably do a poor job, since they are green. If they get too much advice, they are accused of being pawns of the administration.

It also helps in understanding the feeling of one principal who wrote, "Students are simply not in favor of the 'freedoms' they seemingly would like to have, but rather, are extremely interested in a sincere but constant discipline."

Many student activists with whom we spoke were not surprised by the findings of this chapter. Some suggested that most students are cowed by the authority of the principal and, as a result of ignorance about the system and the absence of clear statements concerning their rights, they remain passive. The exaggerated views that students hold of the Ministry's influence suggest that students are indeed ignorant, at least about one important facet of the educational system.

Perhaps one of the problems is that, in the past as well as the present, schools have failed to provide students with sufficient opportunities to learn about the educational system. Few students we have met are familiar with any issues in educational politics, history, sociology, law, or philosophy; and few school curricula offer courses in these areas. The failure of schools to provide students with opportunities to learn about the system in which they spend a major portion of their time may help explain why the students have so little knowledge about that system. It may also help explain why the graduates of our school system are less likely to cast a vote in a school board election than in any other election. One individual with whom we talked, a member of the board of education of a large county, informed us that when he was last elected to office, less than 10% of the eligible voters in the municipality in which he resides bothered to cast a vote. At that time, there were more teachers on the payroll of his board than citizens who cast a vote. One of the traditional objectives of the schools is to promote good citizenship. If a key indicator of good citizenship is voter participation, as many claim, then the schools must be labeled as an abject failure in promoting good citizenship relative to the educational system itself.

Notes

1. The reader can perhaps best recognize this process with respect to women's liberation. The role of the woman in today's society is receiving a great deal of attention, and much debate focuses around differing opinions as to the "most appropriate" role for women.

2. Ontario Department of Education, *Recommendations and Information for Secondary School Organization Leading to Certificates and Diplomas*, Circular H.S.1 (1972/73), p. 9.

3. The reader interested in some general methodological issues is referred to James G. March, "An Introduction to the Theory and Measurement of Influence," *American Political Science Review*, XLIX (June, 1955). Social scientists find the concept of power as confusing as the concept of influence. As Herbert Kaufman and Victor Jones have pointed out in an article called "The Mystery of Power" [*Public Administration Review*, XIV (1954), 205], "There is an elusiveness about power that endows it with an almost ghostly quality. It seems to be all around us, yet this is 'sensed' with some sixth means of reception rather than with the five ordinary senses. We 'know' what it is, yet we encounter endless difficulties in trying to define it. We can 'tell' whether one person or group is more powerful than another, yet we cannot measure power. It is as abstract as time yet as real as a firing squad."

4. Terry N. Clark, "The Concept of Power," in *Community Structure and Decision-Making: Comparative Analyses*, ed. by T. N. Clark (San Francisco: Chandler Publishing, 1968), p. 46.

5. *Ibid.*, p. 47.

6. It should be noted that as a result of a computer programming error, the "don't know" responses for students and SG members were mixed with non-responses. Since non-response rates are generally quite low, however, and since most non-respondents to a particular question probably failed to answer because they did not know, this does not appear to present a serious substantive problem.

7. Student control over course choice was greatly expanded as a result of a Ministry decision. One of the major factors in changes in appearance regulations has probably been student protest activities in Ontario (almost 13% of all student protests reported in our survey revolved around appearance regulations). Regardless of the reasons, some boards have passed policies that greatly restrict the principal's formal authority to impose dress regulations on students. In 1970, for example, the Toronto Board of Education passed the following motion: "Trustee Shanoff, seconded by Trustee Beach, moved, that the matter of appearance of students in the schools, the style of dress and hair, be left to the discretion of the students and parents, except where the health or safety of the student is at stake. The motion was carried" (Minutes of the Toronto Board of Education, February 19, 1970, p. 115). In one school we visited, the principal continues to insist that students dress "properly" – ties and jackets for males and no slacks for females – during assemblies. But even here, the principal has recanted inasmuch as students who do not dress appropriately simply spend their time in the lunchroom or the library during assemblies. Thus, the dress regulation acts essentially as an "admission ticket." Some students in this school indicated that one way to avoid an assembly that does not seem interesting is to wear inappropriate clothing.

8. After our survey was completed, the Minister of Education announced that students would be compelled to take some courses in English and Canadian studies.

3

Student Government Effectiveness

We have two main concerns in this chapter. First, we want to develop an index of student government "effectiveness." Then we want to determine whether the effectiveness of a student government is related to a variety of outcome measures commonly thought to result from good student government. In most schools, a great deal of time and effort is devoted to the organization and administration of the student government. The basic question we want to explore is whether the resources devoted to student government have any payoff.

Since almost all secondary schools in Ontario have some form of student government, it was not possible to answer the question by comparing schools with and without such governments. Therefore, we decided to devise an index of SG effectiveness and to try to determine whether schools with more effective governments were different in any important respects from schools with less effective governments. The hypothesis was that the more effective the student government, the more positive the scores on the various outcome measures. If this were not the case, we might conclude that a large number of staff and students in Ontario secondary schools were wasting their time in trying to make student government in their schools more effective.

An Index of Student Government Effectiveness
How does one judge whether an organization is effective? This question has puzzled social scientists for decades and political philosophers and common observers for millennia. The problem is that the normal response to the question is, "Effective in what way? Effective for whom?" It is hardly a profound observation to note that organizations may be quite effective for the purposes of one group and quite ineffective (indeed, counterproductive) for those of another. The answer to the question depends upon the criteria of effectiveness one uses.

Consider the Watergate affair in the United States. This bizarre series of events led to a great number of editorials in Canadian newspapers applauding the superiority of the parliamentary system of government as practiced in Canada. It was argued that the parliamentary system would have eliminated all of the bitterness, conflict, and general slowdown of government operations in the United States that seemed to result from the protracted Senate hearings, trials, and impeachment proceedings. In a parliamentary system, the government simply would have been dissolved and a new government formed. Proponents of the United States presidential system, however, argue that changing the government is a simple way of hiding dirty laundry. Under the United States system, they claim, the truth has an opportunity to emerge and important legislative reforms have a greater probability of being enacted. Which system is more effective? It depends upon what you most want to accomplish.

Recently, a radical student organization at the University of Toronto (Students for a Democratic Society) physically prevented a controversial professor, Dr. Edward Banfield of the University of Pennsylvania, from delivering a series of lectures at the Toronto campus. One might argue that the student organization was highly effective in this case, because it accomplished its objective. Critics claim, however, that its actions represent a serious threat to academic freedom and endanger the very existence of a university. They suggest further that by choosing an illegitimate means of protesting, the organization has not only threatened the university as an institution, but has discredited itself and thus weakened its ability to accomplish longer-term objectives.

And many people over 30 years of age have been involved in debates over the style of government practiced in the U.S.S.R. Supporters of the system point to the phenomenal industrial growth rate during the Stalin era and the great improvement of living standards for the average citizen in comparison to the centuries of poverty, exploitation, and degradation under the Czars. Critics point to such phenomena as the slaughter of the kulaks, the forced labor camps, and the lack of basic freedoms, and argue that any government that must resort to such measures in order to enforce its will cannot be called really effective.

The concern of this chapter, of course, is not the government systems of large and powerful nation states, or political activities on university campuses, but the very modest forms of student government found in secondary schools. But as is the case with any organization, the problem remains of deciding which criteria are most reasonable for evaluating effectiveness.

One effort at evaluating SG effectiveness was developed in a study conducted by James McPartland and his colleagues at Johns Hopkins University.[1] The McPartland study used a five-item index to evaluate student government. The index required students within a school to indicate whether or not they agreed with the following statements:

1. Student government can change school rules even if teachers and principals are against the changes.
2. Student government does not worry only about the social activities in the school.
3. The teachers and the principal do let students who really disagree with them get elected to student government.
4. Students who are interested in making changes will go to the student government.
5. Members of student government do not necessarily say what will make the teachers and principals happy.

The content of the McPartland items had caused us some concern. We had hoped that some of the findings from our examination of SG effectiveness levels would have policy implications. The individual who is in the strongest position to implement reforms is the principal; for without his cooperation, student governments have little hope of increasing their "legitimate" authority over the areas of student concern. The first McPartland item, "student government can change rules even if teachers and principals are against the changes," is not a characteristic of a student government that would be endorsed by a school principal. On the contrary, a student government that could accomplish school rule changes regardless of the teachers' and the principal's views implies, to most principals, a conflict model – and one in which the power of the students is superior to that of the administration and the teaching staff.[2] To principals this is hardly an endearing quality, and one would not expect them to support, much less foster, such a situation.

If the policy implications of this analysis are to be taken seriously, it seems that a necessary prerequisite is to convince principals that the criteria of effectiveness are ones with which they can agree. If it turns out that their idea of effectiveness conflicts with the ideas of others – students, SG members, directors of education, parents – then these parties will at least have a starting point for intelligent discussion. We decided, then, to use criteria of effectiveness as specified by principals.

Conversation with several principals led us to conclude that some judge SG effectiveness by opinions offered by SG members and teachers, rather than only by students as a whole. One principal, for example, told us that his major criterion would be whether or not SG members felt they could get important changes in the school by working together constructively with teachers and principals. Another principal told us that he judged SG effectiveness by asking teachers if they believed that the student government in their school "represented the feelings of the majority of students." A third principal agreed that the second principal's criterion was important, but he felt that the student body, not the teachers, was the relevant opinion group to ask.

By interviewing a number of principals and reviewing a substantial number of articles and books on student government, we were able to compile a list of potential effectiveness criteria. There was a total of 49 items – all in an agree/disagree format – directed to SG members, to students, and to teachers. Through a survey instrument, every principal in the sample was asked to select the six criteria that he felt "to be most important for the assessment of student government in a school like yours" and to indicate for each of the six items the opinion group to which he would refer the question.

To cover a wide range of dimensions, it was decided to use the eight items most frequently cited by principals as reflecting an effective student government.[3] According to them, a *perfectly* effective student government would be one in which 100% of the SG members agreed that:

1. The decisions made by the student government are for the benefit of the whole school
2. They can almost always get important changes in the school by working together constructively with the principal and teachers

3. They respect the administration
4. They believe the administration respects them
5. Their adviser provides useful support
6. Their experience in student government has increased their appreciation of the value of the democratic process.

In addition, 100% of the student body must agree that:

7. SG members are keeping them informed of important issues under discussion
8. SG members are free to speak their mind rather than saying what will make the teachers and principal happy.

A school in which 100% of the SG members agreed with the first six of their criterion items and 100% of the student body agreed with the last two would rank highest in SG effectiveness. No school scored 100% on all items. The highest was a school that averaged a 93% level of agreement over the six SG member items and a 77% level of agreement over the two student body items. In the lowest-ranked school, SG members averaged a 50% level of agreement over their six items and students averaged a 63% level of agreement over their two items. The weighted mean for the highest school was 89% and for the lowest school, 53%. A similar mean was calculated for all other schools, and they were grouped into five categories. These categories and some pertinent information about each category are presented in table 11.

There are two major issues concerning the index of SG effectiveness. The first is whether or not SG member and student responses to the criterion items are valid. The second relates to the problems of aggregating the individual criterion items into a single index. These issues are discussed below.

Validity of Responses

Since the ranking of schools in terms of SG effectiveness is dependent upon the levels of agreement with the criterion items by students and SG members, the question of the validity of the responses – how accurately they reflect the real situation in the various schools – is important. For example, 72% of the student body in schools that rank highest in SG effectiveness agree that in their schools the "SG members are keeping other students informed about important questions

Table 11/Student Government Member, Student, and Teacher Rankings of Schools in Terms of Student Government Effectiveness

Level of SG Effectiveness	No. of Schools	No. of Respondents		
		SG Members	Students	Teachers
Highest	5	64	342	195
Second highest	6	122	394	224
Third highest	12	280	809	416
Fourth highest	9	205	866	472
Lowest	5	134	356	219

that are being discussed," while in schools with the least effective government only 33% of the student body agree. Are these two groups of schools really different? One means of checking their responses is to look at teachers' perceptions of the same situation. If both students and teachers agree in their perceptions of conditions in a school, we may conclude that the differences between schools with high and low SG effectiveness are not artificial and based upon students' misperceptions.

We find that teacher responses generally parallel student responses in rating SG effectiveness. Table 12 presents the responses of SG members or students (the percentage that agrees with each statement) for each of the criterion items and the teacher responses to the same questions, comparing schools rated as highest in

Table 12/Percentage Agreement of Student Government Member or Student Responses and Teacher Responses to Student Government Effectiveness Criteria in Schools Rated as Highest and Lowest in Effectiveness

	SG Members or Students		Teachers	
Criteria	Highest SG Effect.	Lowest SG Effect.	Highest SG Effect.	Lowest SG Effect.
SG Members				
1. Decisions made by the student government are for the benefit of the whole school	95	72	85	59
2. SG members can almost always get important changes in the school by working together constructively with the principal and teachers	83	63	81	81
3. SG members respect the administration	94	74	88	71
4. The administration respects SG members	97	73	93	82
5. The faculty adviser provides useful support to the student government	81	67		
6. My SG experience has increased my appreciation of the value of the democratic process	49	80		
Students				
7. SG members keep students informed of important issues under discussion	72	43	70	33
8. SG members are free to speak their mind rather than saying what will make the teachers and principal happy	75	73	73	70

effectiveness with those rated as lowest. Of the eight effectiveness criteria, six were presented to teachers.[4] Of these six, teachers' responses closely parallel student or SG member responses in four cases, numbers 1, 3, 4, and 7. The two items where teachers' responses do not parallel student responses both refer to interactions between students and teachers. We suspect that there is a bias in teachers' responses to these questions; that is, as part of their own professional role identity, teachers are likely to think of themselves as open to working constructively with students (number 2) and providing an atmosphere in which students will say what they think without fear of punishment (number 8), whatever may be the real situation in the school as seen by the students. But in the four items where teachers were asked to judge general conditions in their school rather than their own behavior and attitudes, their responses discriminate between schools with very effective and very ineffective student governments in the same way as do student and SG member responses.

Aggregation
One problem created by the use of the average level of agreement across the eight criterion items to classify schools is that such aggregation does not capture perfectly all the variations in responses to the eight criteria, item by item. Schools categorized as least effective, for example, are not necessarily lowest on each criterion; note that the levels of agreement in the highest-ranked and the lowest-ranked schools are nearly identical for item number 8 (although the small difference does favor the more effective student governments). This problem is particularly severe in the three middle categories of effectiveness. Consider item number 4, "the administration respects SG members." The level of agreement in most effective schools is 24% higher than in least effective schools. The level of agreement in fourth-ranked schools is higher, however, than in third-ranked schools. Thus, this complex measure of SG effectiveness produces very clear distinctions only at the extremes, and there is much overlapping in the three middle categories.

For the most part, the analysis that follows is restricted to comparisons of these extreme groups. For simplicity, schools in the highest category are referred to as effective student government (ESG) schools, and those in the lowest category, ineffective student government (ISG) schools. SG effectiveness as defined by the principals' criteria is examined in relation to some major functions of student government and other effectiveness criteria.

Student Government as a Democratic Organization Representing a Constituency
Most student governments in Ontario are viewed by the principals as a means of demonstrating to students democratic procedures, processes, structures, and principles. The selection of delegates is often preceded by campaign speeches and posters. On election day, each student casts a ballot. Parliamentary procedure is followed in a number of schools; and constitutions, where they exist, outline the structure, aims, and duties of the student government. In some cases, student governments are organized on the parliamentary model, with a Prime Minister, Opposition Party, and so on.

Most SG constitutions charge the student government with the responsibility of representing student opinions and student grievances to the administration. One constitution states that an "aim" of the student council is "to provide a responsible organization to represent the student body and to act on its behalf." Another constitution describes one of the functions of the Cabinet (a subgroup of student council) as follows: "They shall meet with the Administration regularly to consider plans and student grievances as brought forward by the Student Council or themselves."

To be sure, there still exist constitutions that place severe restrictions on student governments. One, for example, reads: "The student council will not concern itself with matters of school policy." But even in the school that produced this constitutional constraint, students were petitioning for changes in dress regulations and pressing for smoking privileges.

A democratic system that can competently represent the people has a number of characteristics of which three in particular stand out: the constituency's perceptions of the selection mechanism, the communication between representatives and their constituency, and the structure of influence. Constituency (students') perceptions and in some cases teachers' perceptions of these characteristics are examined in the context of effective student government as defined by principals.

The Selection Mechanism
In all jurisdictions citizens complain about the selection mechanism. They say, "The only way to enter politics is to be wealthy. The wealthy get in office, not the true leaders"; or, "In order to run for office, you have to know the right people."

It may not take wealth or influence to enter student government, but (as we demonstrate in Chapter 4) there do appear to be biases operating in the selection mechanism for SG representatives. One of the problems in the secondary system is that many principals fail to recognize the complexity of the social structure contained in their school. In most schools, there are a large number of different cliques, which have different concerns and statuses. In general, student governments are relatively homogeneous and therefore do not have highly developed communication lines open with all groups of students. It is this state of affairs that partially explains the problems of one Ontario school described by Alexander A. Kovaloff:

School cliques were a big problem for the student council in an eastern area high school. The school was composed of Indian, rural and urban students. Each group was loyal to its own members and therefore the student council had difficulty in creating activities which would involve the whole school. One activity, acceptable to the rural group, would not be acceptable to the other two. The individual groups refused to mix with each other.[5]

In any political system, it would be ideal if the true leaders were the elected leaders and if the true leaders were also the most politically talented. When Ontario students were asked whether or not "SG members are the *true leaders* of the students in this school," the majority (65%) answered in the negative.[6] There is, however, a substantial difference between ESG and ISG schools. In the latter schools, 70% of the students said that the "SG members are *not* the true leaders of the students," while 49% of the students so responded in the former schools. The situation, then, is far better in ESG schools, but even they still have a long way to go.

It may be that in schools the qualities of leadership and political ability do not go hand in hand and that the student body, in its wisdom, chooses those who are politically skillful rather than those who are true leaders. But if such is the case, it is not so perceived by the students. Sixty-nine percent of the student body disagree that "SG members represent the best political skills among the students in this school." In ISG schools, 74% of the student body disagree; and in ESG schools, 62% disagree. While ESG schools are superior, a substantial majority of students in all categories of schools believe that students with the most political talent are not representing them. Moreover, this belief is shared by 81% of the teachers in ISG schools and 65% of the teachers in ESG schools.

When specific types of people are not found in a political organization, sometimes the reason is that they choose not to run and at other times it is that they are excluded from running. The perceptions of students provide support for the second reason, at least with respect to students who have basic disagreements with the principal or teachers in a school. In ISG schools, 88% of the students agree that "the teachers and principals do *not* let students who strongly disagree with them run for student government in this school." Even in ESG schools, 78% of the student body agree that the principal and teachers would block students from running for student government if these students had strong disagreements with the principal and his staff.[7] Perhaps this explains why about two-thirds of the student body believe that "student government in this school is just a tool of the administration." Interestingly, a slightly greater percentage (6% more) of both students and teachers in ESG schools feels that this statement is true.

Communication

Regardless of who serves as a student representative, the role itself carries certain expectations. The incumbent is expected to represent the feelings of the majority; and to do so, he must establish and maintain communication with the student body. The principals in our survey selected an item that deals with communication between student government and students as one of their criteria for SG effectiveness, namely, "SG members should keep other students informed about important questions that are being discussed." In ESG schools, a greater percentage of students believes that the student government does keep students informed. Twenty-two percent more students in ESG schools also agree that "SG members in this school try to find out from other students which issues should be raised at SG meetings" (71% and 49% in ESG and ISG schools, respectively). In view of the students' low opinion of the selection mechanism, it is surprising to note that, in ISG schools, 69% of the students agree that "the student government represents the feelings of the *majority* of students in this school" (in ESG schools, 75% of the student body agree). It is also somewhat surprising to note that a majority of students in ISG schools agrees that "the student government deals with the issues students view as the most important in this school" (59% of the students in ISG schools and 73% of the students in ESG schools agree).

Student Government Influence as Perceived by Students
A majority of students believe that SG representatives are neither their "true leaders" nor the "politically most talented," and that student council members are "tools of the administration." Yet most students also believe that the "student government represents the feelings of the majority" and that its members "deal with the issues students view as the most important." The apparent contradiction in these perceptions is partly explained by the fact that many students believe that the student government in their school does not have "all the influence it needs to represent the students properly" (58% of the students so responded). In other words, it seems that students perceive their student government as understanding and dealing with the issues; but because it lacks sufficient influence, it is unable to transform this understanding into concrete decisions that result in changes. Dealing with issues is, after all, a far cry from dealing effectively with issues.

Students perceive effective student governments as having more influence. In ESG schools, 54% of the student body (as compared with 39% in ISG schools) agree that "student government in this school has all the influence it needs to represent the students properly." Teachers' perceptions tend to confirm the students' opinions. In ESG schools, 57%, and in ISG schools, 51% of the teachers agree with this statement. But the greatest consensus among teachers is the belief that the student government in their school "is passive." More teachers in ESG than in ISG schools hold this view – 82% and 70%, respectively.

To summarize, then, it appears that from the students' point of view, effective student governments are superior in that they are more likely (1) to be represented by both the "true leaders of the school" and the most "politically skillful," (2) to represent the feelings of the majority and deal with the issues that students view as most important, (3) to possess all of the influence they need to properly represent the students.

There is some question, however, as to whether or not effective student governments actually exercise the additional influence they are believed to possess. In ESG schools, a greater percentage of students believes that "student government is a tool of the administration" and a greater percentage of teachers believes that the student government in their school "is passive."

It is also worth emphasizing that even in those cases where effective student governments fare better than ineffective student governments, they are still far from an "ideal state." A majority of students from ESG schools believes that (1) SG members do not represent the best political skills among students in the school (62%), (2) teachers and principals do not let students who strongly disagree with them run for student government (78%), (3) SG members are just a tool of the administration (70%).

A majority of teachers in ESG schools believes that (1) SG members do not represent the best political skills among students in the school (65%), (2) the student government is passive (82%).

Furthermore, a substantial minority of students in ESG schools believes that (1) SG members are not the true leaders of students in their schools (49%), (2) student government does *not* have all the influence it needs to represent the students properly (46%).

A substantial minority (42%) of teachers in ESG schools also agrees that "student government does *not* have all the influence it needs to represent the students properly."

Principals' Perceptions of Student Government Influence

One of the criteria of an effective student government focused on the degree to which SG members felt they could get important changes in the school by working constructively with the principal, vice-principal, or teachers. By definition, then, members of effective student governments feel more influential than do their counterparts in ineffective student governments.

In this section, the views of the principals are examined in order to answer two questions:
1. Do principals of ESG schools, as compared to principals of ISG schools, believe that their student government has a greater degree of influence?
2. Is there a difference in the means by which effective and ineffective student governments participate in the decision-making process?

To answer the first question, principals were asked how much influence they believe their student government has over each of the 10 decision areas discussed in Chapter 2. Their answers ranged across a four-point scale: 1, no influence, 2, a little influence, 3, moderate influence, and 4, a lot of influence. Over all decision areas, principals of ESG schools gave their student governments an influence score of 2.5, midway between a little and a moderate amount of influence. Principals of ISG schools gave their student governments an average score of 1.9, slightly lower than a little influence. On a scale of 1 to 4, a difference of 0.6 is quite substantial. There is little doubt that the principals of ESG schools perceive their student government as possessing more influence.

Of course, it could be argued that a measure of SG influence such as that just used ignores the distributive dimension of influence – that is, a group's influence can be understood only in relative terms because influence is distributed, usually unequally, among different institutions or individuals. For example, assume that both student government A and student government B are ranked, by the principal, as possessing a great deal of influence over decision x. Using the influence measure described in the previous paragraph, one would have to conclude that they are viewed by their respective principals as equally influential. Also assume, however, that the principal of student government A indicates that he personally possesses a great deal of influence over decision x, while the principal of student government B indicates that he possesses no influence over decision x. One is now led to a different conclusion, namely, that other things being equal, student government B is perceived as being *more* influential than student government A.

Because there are only 10 schools in the ESG and ISG school categories and therefore only 10 principals, the distributive characteristic of influence could make a substantial difference. Thus, it was decided to recompute the SG influence scores, this time holding the principals' influence level constant. For ease of analysis, SG influence was calculated only for decisions in which the principal felt he personally exercised a lot of influence. These accounted for about 75% of all the decision areas.[8] The results of this calculation not only support but strengthen the previous conclusion – that effective student governments are perceived by the principals as possessing more influence than ineffective student governments. Principals of ESG schools rated their student governments at 2.7 (3.0 is a moderate amount of influence), while principals of ISG schools rated them with a 2.0 average (a little influence).

The difference between the overall influence score of effective and ineffective student governments is a function of two variables: the scope of influence and the degree of influence. The scope of a person's or group's influence refers to the range of decisions over which influence is exercised. Thus, if student governments A and B exercise a great deal of influence in every significant decision in which they participate, but student government A participates in a greater number of significant decisions, then student government A is viewed as more influential. Looking only at those decision areas over which the principal exercises a great deal of influence, we see that effective student governments exercise at least some influence in 78% of the decision areas, while ineffective student governments exercise at least some influence in 61% of the decision areas – a difference in "scope" of 17%.

As well as having a greater scope of influence, effective student governments have a greater degree of influence. Principals in ESG schools score the governments at 3.1 (slightly above a moderate amount of influence) in those decisions over which they have at least some influence, as compared to a 2.6 score given by principals of ISG schools (midway between a little and a moderate amount of influence).

Having established that effective student governments are perceived, by their principals, as possessing a greater degree of influence over a greater range of decisions, we are next faced with the problem of defining the means by which these student governments exercise their greater influence.

Neither principals nor other opinion groups were asked to specify how student governments exercise their influence within the formal decision-making structure of the school; but principals were asked what they believed to be the most preferable method of student participation in each decision area. Should students have complete control, share formal authority with the principal or staff, or give their views to the principal or teachers who will then make the final decision? Presumably, principals satisfy their personal preferences in cases where they have the power to do so; and it is probable that they do have the power in decision areas where they perceive themselves as having a great deal of influence. These high-influence decision areas were analyzed in an effort to determine how student governments exercise influence. (We eliminated from the analysis decisions in which the principal said that the student government has no influence, for in these cases the question of method of participation is irrelevant.)

In Chapter 2, it was shown that principals do not favor complete student control over any decision area except student course choices and appearance rules. It is in these two areas also where principals are most likely to define their own influence as modest. We therefore did not expect that principals of ESG schools would describe their student government as possessing complete control over any decision area of high principal influence, and the data bear this expectation out.

A second method by which student governments may exercise influence is by sharing authority over specific decisions with the principal or the teachers. Such sharing of power is a relatively rare occurrence in schools. In North York's MAGU (Multi-Age Grouping Unit) school, however, student representatives have an equal voice in a wide range of school decisions, including the sensitive area of hiring new teachers. Of course, MAGU is a relatively small, highly experimental school. John Adams High School in Portland, Oregon – a school of 1,300 students – is more typical of the "average" Ontario secondary school. According to John Geurnsey, an education writer for the Portland *Oregonian*:

One of the most innovative changes at Adams is in the area of school policy-making. While the ultimate responsibility for the operation of the school rests with the principal, Adams is experimenting with a mechanism to permit majority rule voting by students and faculty members on some issues. The Adams operation duplicates in some respects the functioning of the U.S. Government.

The principal of Adams argues that "the whole issue of decision-making in conventional high schools is wrong. The students and faculty members want more voice, so we're experimenting with the delegation of authority."[9]

There are cases where principals share authority with students. Also, as stated in Chapter 2, a few principals indicate a preference for sharing authority with students in at least some decision areas. We expected that these principals would be found in the ESG schools, for it is in these schools that the principal imputes greater influence to the student government. The data do not, however, support this expectation. In ESG schools, only one principal indicates a preference for shared authority, and he does so for two decision areas: student discipline and student grading. In ISG schools, two principals indicate a preference for shared authority, and they do so for one decision area each: student grading and appearance rules.

There is, then, no evidence that differences exist between ESG and ISG schools regarding the delegation of formal authority by principals to the student government. To the degree that student governments exercise any influence at all within the formal structure, they do so by providing information, ideas, or opinions either directly or indirectly to the principal.[10] Presumably, then, the greater influence of effective student governments is a function, not of the decision-making structure, but of the interpersonal relationship that exists between their members and the principal. It seems likely that the relationship is characterized by variation in the principal's willingness to listen to and carefully weigh the ideas of students and perhaps by the quality of the student government's input. One important point to note, however, is that while the relationship between the principal and the student government in an ESG school seems to be characterized by stronger feelings of mutual respect, the principal in this type of school seems no more willing to grant decision-making responsibilities to students. One principal of an ESG school explained it this way:

Although I think that students should be given as much responsibility for decision-making in regard to dress, smoking, eating areas, choice of courses, discipline, new courses, political activity, etc., I find that:
a) many students do not want this responsibility;
b) many students do not have the background of knowledge and experience sufficient to make valid judgements and wise decisions;
c) in some cases choice of courses decisions are made on superficial reasons such as no examinations, no homework required, etc., regardless of the real value of the course for future needs. However, many students are more mature and make the wise choice. This is also applied to opinions re smoking, etc. For some students their own personal desires are paramount and the rights and desires of others are not considered.

A principal of an ISG school explained his position as follows:

There is but one major issue in the area of decision-making; who is going to run the ship? Children are simply not capable of making the far-reaching decisions so why put these things into the hands of immature, inexperienced infants, however, intelligent.

The attitudes of the two principals are different, but the position of their student governments within the formal decision-making structure is similar: neither shares authority nor formally participates in any of the important decision-making processes within the school.

Fostering School Spirit Through Extracurricular Activities
Almost every student government is charged with the responsibility of fostering school spirit. In most cases, the vehicles used to promote school spirit are the financing and promotion of extracurricular activities and the organization and promotion of special events (such as winter carnivals or activity days). Dances constitute one of the most popular and often one of the most troublesome events. Controversies focus on such issues as whether or not students from outside the school should be allowed into the dances, how much money should be spent for a dance band, and in some cases whether or not liquor should be served to those over 18 years of age if the dance is to be held outside the school.

Besides dances, schools offer a variety of extracurricular activities ranging from athletic programs to special subject clubs. In one case study school, the only collective decision the student government made during the entire year was the allocation of funds to these clubs and programs. In other schools, however, student governments may set an "activity fee" and decide who should pay and how much. Some student governments also are active in the creation of new extracurricular activities, in promoting student participation in existing activities, and in supervising the organization and administration of such activities.

The first question to be addressed, then, is whether or not effective student governments contribute to increased student participation in these extracurricular activities. Students were asked whether or not they engaged in extracurricular activities in their school. A greater percentage of students from ESG schools does engage in extracurricular activities – 82% from the schools rated most effective, as compared to about 70% from all other schools. When one examines the amount of time students spend in extracurricular activities, however, it appears that most of the variation is explained by activities that consume very little time. Thirty-one percent of the students in ESG schools spend more than three hours a week in extracurricular activities, while 27% of the students in the ISG schools spend more than three hours a week – a difference of only 4%.

The patterns of student participation (proportions of participants who take part in various kinds of activities) are similar for all schools, regardless of the effectiveness of their student government, except for intramural athletics. Forty-eight percent of all students in ESG schools participate in intramural athletics, while 37% of the students participate in ISG schools. A student can claim to be a member of an intramural team by engaging in a sport for a few hours a month. This activity probably explains why the participation rate of students in ESG schools is higher, while the percentage of students who spend more than three hours a week in school activities is about the same as in ISG schools.

When students were asked why they do not spend more time in extracurricular activities, they offered a variety of responses. Understandably, more students in ESG schools say they already spend a lot of time – 19% as compared to 11.4% for students in ISG schools. There is, however, no single category of responses that explains the lower participation rates in ISG schools. These schools have about 3% more students who say they must work after school, 3% more who claim that it is difficult to get a ride home after school, about 1.5% more who say, "I have better things to do," and about the same percentage who have other reasons. In both ESG and ISG schools, the same percentage of students state that they do not participate because they do not have friends. This percentage, however, is extremely small – just over 3% in both sets of schools.

It has been argued that participation in school activities leads to a feeling of involvement and that this is the essence of school spirit. It does appear to be the case that participation and feelings of involvement go hand in hand. Twice the percentage of students in ESG schools report feeling very involved in the school. But the percentage of students who express this sentiment is low in all schools. Only 12% of the students in ESG schools and 6% of the students in ISG schools report that they feel very involved. In ESG schools, 28% of the students say they are not at all involved, while 40% of the students in ISG schools claim to be not at all involved. Although ESG schools do better in generating feelings of high involvement, even their success is limited to a small fraction of the student body.

The most dramatic variations between ESG and ISG schools arise, not in differences in the student body, but in differences between SG members and between SG members and students in ESG schools. Looking at the same items for student government as were just described for students, we conclude that an effective student government is more successful in fostering its own school spirit than in fostering the school spirit of the student body.

In the highest-ranked schools, 92% of the SG members spend more than three hours a week in SG work or some other extracurricular activity, as compared to 40% to 50% for all other schools. (Recall that 31% and 27%, respectively, of the student body in ESG and ISG schools spend more than three hours a week.) While ESG schools do have a greater participation rate than other schools, the greatest variation is *within* these schools: 61% more SG members than students spend more than three hours a week in school activities, a difference that is greater than that between ESG and ISG schools.

Understandably, when the SG members from the highest-ranked schools were asked why they do not spend more time in extracurricular activities, 67% of them said that they already spent sufficient time in school activities, as compared to 35% to 40% of SG members in the other schools. No SG members in the former schools reported that they had better things to do, but 14% of the members in the lowest-ranked schools gave this response.

There is a tendency for a greater percentage of the ESG members to engage in other extracurricular activities. This is particularly true of publications activities – newspapers and yearbooks – where 38% of them spend time as compared to 18% of the ISG members. Close to 20% more of the ESG members also engage in intramural athletics and serve on social committees.

As indicated earlier, there does seem to be a positive relationship between participation in school activities and feelings of being involved in the school. For ESG members, participation includes a greater variety of activities as well as a greater time commitment. (Recall that only 12% of the student body in ESG schools feel very involved in the school and the 52% of SG members who report feeling very involved becomes truly astounding.) Only one ESG member (of 64 respondents) reported feeling not at all involved. While one out of two ESG members says that he is very involved, only one out of four in all other schools expresses this feeling. In the school with the least effective student government, 20% of its SG members say they are not at all involved in the school.

There is, then, some evidence that ESG schools are also schools with the highest rates of student participation in extracurricular activities. Further, these same schools have the greatest percentage of students who feel very involved in the school. The survey data that we have collected do not provide us with sufficient evidence to draw conclusions as to why this association exists. It could be that the student government is truly more successful in promoting extracurricular activities and therefore directly contributes to greater participation. Or it could be that some extraneous factors – the personal style of the principal or the social characteristics of the students – explain the positive attitudes of the SG members, their high participation rates, and their feelings of involvement, as well as the higher student body participation rate. Finally, it is possible that the extraordinary activity and enthusiasm of the SG members have a spin-off effect and that the marginally higher participation rates of the student body in these schools over those in other schools are a result of a contagious force generated by the activity of the SG members themselves.

Student Influence in Extracurricular Activities
One of the major areas in which students have a potential opportunity to learn about decision-making is in extracurricular activities. During recent teachers'

work-to-rule campaigns, a number of principals temporarily terminated a wide range of extracurricular activities. In some schools, however, students were permitted to operate these activities independently. While no systematic research has been conducted on this topic, the authors have had the opportunity to discuss with a number of students the experience of operating extracurricular activities. Through these conversations, it is evident that the students are thoroughly enjoying their new responsibilities and believe that they are deriving as much benefit from operating the activity as they are from participating in it.

Students who claimed membership in various extracurricular activities were asked who controlled most things in the activity – "adult advisers," "some of the students," or "my friends and I." In only two classes of activities, musical groups and interscholastic athletics, do more than 50% of student members perceive adult advisers as controlling most things. Since both of these are skill-oriented, training-based activities, this figure is hardly surprising. Indeed, what might be considered surprising is that just over 20% of the students who compete in interscholastic athletics and just over 30% of members of musical groups perceive that adults do not control most things. Among the various specified activities, those with the lowest percentages of perceived adult control are publications groups, hobby clubs, social activity committees, and prefect societies, in all of which less than one-third of student members see adults as controlling most things.

From a pedagogical point of view, these may be regarded as fairly positive indications. If one assumes, as we do, that students learn to make decisions by having the opportunity to make them and that they learn to exercise responsible control over their affairs by actually controlling situations, it would appear that it is in these extracurricular activities that students are gaining this experience.

This optimistic interpretation must, however, be balanced against two other facts. First, with the exception of athletics (where student control percentages are low), membership percentages for these extracurricular activities are low. Thus, many students do not have the opportunity to exercise control. Moreover, when the two "student control" responses are considered – "some of the students" and "my friends and I" control most things – it appears that a majority of members (3.4 times as many for all activities) see other students rather than themselves as being in control. In only one category, hobby clubs, does this ratio fall below 2:1. Thus, although in most activities the majority of members do not see adults in control, few students have a sense of personal control.

Along this dimension, there is little difference between ESG and ISG schools. A slightly higher percentage of students who participate in extracurricular activities in ESG schools, as compared to participants in ISG schools, perceives adult advisers as controlling most things. This situation would appear to be accounted for by the fact that participation rates in intramural athletics, where overall adult control responses are relatively high, are slightly higher in ESG schools.

Student Satisfaction with School Life

Although student governments may not be able directly to influence many sources of student dissatisfaction with school (for example, poorly taught courses or personality conflicts with teachers or other students), they can affect many potential sources of dissatisfaction (such as extracurricular activities or personal behavior and dress regulations). Moreover, it can be argued that students who believe they have an effective voice representing their interests in areas where they desire change are more likely to find their life in school satisfying than those who do not.

Students were first asked how much satisfaction (a lot, some, very little, or none) they got from five basic areas of school life: school courses, athletics, clubs and plays, relationships with teachers, and relationships with the administration. There are no differences between schools, regardless of the effectiveness of their student government, for any areas except relationships with teachers. In ESG schools, 59% of the student body indicate that they receive a lot or some satisfaction from student/teacher relationships while 52% of the student body in ISG schools concur. While the difference is statistically significant there is only a 7% difference. However, looking at more detailed questions on student/teacher relationships reveals more substantial differences.

Almost twice as many students (25% as compared to 13%) in ESG than in ISG schools believe that most or all of their teachers listen to their opinions with genuine interest. Moreover, there is a considerable difference in the percentage of students who feel that there is at least one teacher with whom they can discuss personal problems; 71% of the students in ESG schools say that there is one or more such teacher in their school, while only half of the students in ISG schools concur. There is, however, no substantial difference in the percentage of students who feel that teachers treat them as equals. Only a quarter of the students from all schools believe that most or all of their teachers treat them as equals.

Students were then asked how they felt about a range of more specific areas in their school, many of which are frequent topics of conversation and complaint among SG members and students alike. The areas are:

1. School rules about dress codes
2. School rules about smoking
3. Other school rules, such as hall passes, where students may eat their lunches
4. School rules about outside speakers and assemblies, unofficial leaflets and newspapers, student meetings, and political rallies
5. The way courses are taught
6. The types of courses given
7. The way cafeteria service is handled
8. The way each student is assigned to (or permitted to choose) courses
9. The way students are disciplined
10. The way students are graded
11. The kinds of dances and social activities held.

Students were asked to rate each area as 1, very bad; 2, bad; 3, moderate; 4, good; or 5, very good. Students in ESG schools as compared to those in ISG schools believe that, on the average, these areas are slightly better in their schools. How much of this results from the student government and how much results from the principal cannot be determined. But one principal in an ESG school informed us that, for his school, our questions regarding influence over appearance rules, smoking rules, and even school rules were irrelevant. Next to these items, he wrote "we don't care," suggesting that there are no restrictive rules at all in these areas. Furthermore, this school is relatively large, having over 1,500 students. If it were a small school, social pressure could serve as a workable substitute to formal rules for keeping students "in line."

In other areas as well, students in ESG schools express a slightly higher level of positive feelings toward their school. About 6% more agree that students in their school are not treated like children (79% and 73%, respectively, in ESG and ISG schools), and almost twice the percentage of students in ESG schools feel that life in school is very exciting or pretty exciting (35% as compared to 18% in ISG schools). In addition, teachers in ESG schools perceive the student body as being substantially more satisfied with school life than do teachers in ISG schools. Seventy-four percent of the teachers in the highest-ranked schools estimate that three-quarters of the student body are very satisfied or pretty satisfied, as compared to 51% to 61% of teachers from all other categories of schools. Thus, while teachers seem to have an exaggerated view of student satisfaction, they are able to sense the differences between schools.[11]

In general then, students in ESG schools feel that specific rules and policies in their schools are better, they are less likely to feel that they are treated like children, and they are more likely to find life in school exciting. They do not differ from students in ISG schools in terms of their satisfaction with school courses, athletics, clubs and plays, or relationships with the administration. However, they are moderately more satisfied with their general relationship with teachers. They are much more likely to feel that there is one or more teacher with whom they can discuss a personal problem, and that most or all of their teachers listen to their opinions with genuine interest. When it comes to feelings about teachers treating them as equals, though, they do not feel more positively toward teachers than do their counterparts in ISG schools.

Summary and Conclusion

To Ontario secondary school principals, a perfectly effective student government can be characterized as follows: first, students have elected representatives who feel free to speak their own mind; and second, the representatives have developed a relationship of mutual respect with the principal – a relationship that has been facilitated by a faculty adviser who also provides *all* of the necessary support to the student government.

This truly effective student government has developed a mechanism to keep students informed of important issues that are under discussion. From their relationships with the principal and their faculty adviser, SG members have come to feel that not only can they speak their minds, but they can also effect important changes by working cooperatively with the principal and his staff. They make decisions only after considering the well-being of the entire school. Moreover, the entire SG experience is an exercise in democracy; and when SG members complete their terms of office, they feel a greater appreciation of the value of the democratic process.

Of the schools in our sample, only five approximated the principal's conception of a perfectly effective student government. The question is, how do the students and SG members perceive these so-called effective student governments?

Students who are represented by an effective student government have a tendency to agree that their student council is composed of the true student leaders and the most politically skillful, and that their representatives represent the feelings of the majority and deal with those issues that students view as most important. Furthermore, these students are likely to perceive their student government as possessing all of the influence it needs to represent them properly. However, they tend to express skepticism concerning the use that their student government makes of its influence; specifically, a slightly greater percentage of students from ESG schools than those from ISG schools believes that the student government is "a tool of the administration."

A greater percentage of students from ESG schools participate in at least one extracurricular activity, but there is very little difference between them and students from ISG schools in terms of the amount of time spent in such activities. Further, students in ESG schools do not view themselves as having any greater influence over decisions made in extracurricular activities. There is, however, a difference in their feelings of involvement – 12% more students from ISG schools feel totally uninvolved in their school.

Students in ESG schools feel that specific rules and policies in their school are better, they are less likely to feel that they are treated like children, and they are more likely to find life in school exciting than is the case with students in other schools. They are also likely to believe that teachers listen to their opinions with genuine interest and that there are at least some teachers with whom they can discuss personal problems.

In general, then, when one compares students from ESG and ISG schools, the former seem to have more positive views. While many of the differences are not great, they are fairly consistent. When one compares these students to an "ideal" state, however, it becomes clear that even ESG schools have a long way to go. Even in ESG schools, 78% of the student body believe that students who have strong disagreements with principals or teachers will be excluded from running for student government; 62% of the students (and 65% of the teachers) believe that students with the best political skills are not SG members; and 46% of the students (and 42% of the teachers) believe the student government needs more influence if it is properly to represent the student body.

While almost twice as many students from ESG schools as compared to those from ISG schools believe that most or all of their teachers listen to their opinions with genuine interest, 75% of them feel that this is not the case. Again, while almost twice as many students from ESG schools feel that life in school is very or pretty exciting, 65% of these students feel that life in school is either ordinary or boring.

Those student governments that are defined by the principals' criteria as the most effective are, at the same time, characterized by 82% of the teachers as "passive" student governments and by 70% of the students as "tools of the administration." These characterizations may stem, in part at least, from the role of student governments in the decision-making structure. While the principals of ESG schools describe the government as being more influential over a greater range of decisions, they do not grant their student government any greater formal authority. Principals of ESG and ISG schools share similar attitudes on the role that student government does and should play in the decision-making process, namely, an advisory role rather than a sharing of authority. In the advisory role, student governments propose and the principals dispose. In effective student governments, the student government is permitted and perhaps even encouraged to propose over a greater range of issues, and the principal seems more likely to consider these proposals carefully in making his final decision.

But the greatest difference between ESG and ISG schools arises, not so much in the feelings of the student body, but in the attitudes of the SG members themselves. ESG members spend a substantially greater amount of time in a wider range of school activities, and possess an extraordinarily high degree of positive feelings about, and commitment to, their respective schools, as contrasted with ISG members. The pedagogical consequences of their SG experience are discussed in the following chapter. Suffice it to say here, that, with some important exceptions (mainly in the crucial area of decision-making), these students also seem to have more positive learning experiences than do their ISG counterparts.

From the data presented in this chapter, it is possible to reach a few conclusions – some definite, but most tentative. The most definite conclusion that can be drawn is that the principals' conception of SG effectiveness ignores a number of critical perceptions, particularly certain perceptions of students and teachers. This, in turn, has two implications. First, a student government regarded by the principal as highly effective may fail to meet the students' expectations as a constituency and may appear to operate in a very undemocratic system, particularly with respect to the selection mechanism. Second, many principals (particularly in large schools) have their greatest student contact with SG members and hence are likely to assume that the attitudes of their student body are reflected by the attitudes of their student government. It seems clear, however, that such generalizations are very risky. As evidenced by the data on effective student governments, those with extremely positive views and strong school commitments do not necessarily reflect the views and commitments of the student body in general. Principals, then, would be advised to distinguish carefully between the attitudes and the commitments of their student government and the attitudes and commitments of their student body.

It does appear that there is a relationship between SG effectiveness and many positive attitudes of the student body. It is also possible, however, that these associations are best explained by the style and personality of the principal rather than the perspicacity or efficacy of the student government. This would also tend to explain the fact that the variations between effective and ineffective student governments are so much greater than the variations between student bodies. The impact of a single individual's personality – unless it is absolutely charismatic – is strongest over those with whom he has personal and sustained contact. SG members are more likely than other students to have frequent contact with the principal and therefore are more likely to be affected by his personality and leadership style.

One other conclusion that can be stated is that, while SG influence may vary between schools, there is very little variation in the degree of formal authority possessed by student governments, at least in the 10 decision areas investigated. The fact that virtually all student governments are devoid of formal authority suggests that even ESG members do not have the opportunity to participate in the total decision-making process and certainly do not have a chance to deal with the increasing responsibility that comes with increased authority. Because effective student governments do not possess any greater share of formal authority than ineffective student governments, it is not possible to provide evidence concerning the possible consequences on students', student governments', or teachers' attitudes or actions as a result of alterations in the formal decision-making structure. It does seem clear, however, that an alteration in the decision-making structure of the school is a policy decision that could be made to effect a gradual increase in SG authority. Thus far, principals have avoided experimenting with this type of structural reform.

Notes

1. James McPartland et al., *Student Participation in High School Decisions: A Study of 14 Urban High Schools*, Final Report, Project No. 9-0163, January, 1971 (Baltimore, Md.: Center for Social Organization of Schools, Johns Hopkins University, 1971).

2. The authors may have intended a model of shared authority over school rules in which student government held a majority of the voting power; but, as evident from our earlier discussion on student influence, the shared authority model is not a popular one in Ontario secondary schools. Only two of the 36 principals surveyed would sanction "students and staff both voting," and only one believed students should have complete control over school rules.

3. A different evaluation technique was used to provide direct feedback to schools on the effectiveness of their student government. This technique, called the "critical decision method," did not generate a single set of criteria but provided information based on each principal's unique set of six criteria chosen from the list of 49 possible criteria. Each principal also provided, for each criterion he selected, an a priori statement as to the variable states that would constitute a problem (that is, his critical decision range). Thus, a critical decision range was defined according to the logic of March and Simon's concept of "satisficing" (James G. March and Herbert A. Simon, *Organizations* [New York: John Wiley and Sons, 1967], pp. 140–141). The actual data were then compared to the principal's critical decision range to determine if a problem existed. Effective student governments were those with no problems, while the least effective student governments had six problems, one on each criterion. See W. E. Alexander and J. P. Farrell, "The Effectiveness of Student Governments in Ontario Secondary Schools," A Report to Principals (Toronto: Department of Educational Planning, Ontario Institute for Studies in Education, November 1973).

4. The other two were judged inappropriate for teachers. One, number 5, would have asked them to evaluate a specific identified teaching colleague (the SG adviser). The other, number 6, would have required teachers to judge the attitudinal changes of SG members – a characteristic not likely to be visible to most teachers.

5. Alexander A. Kovaloff, "A Report on the Central Ontario Zac Phimister Student Leadership Conference," June 20–23, 1971 at Queen's University, Kingston, Ontario, p. 24.

6. Even SG representatives recognize that they are not the "true leaders"; 60% of the SG members also answered in the negative.

7. SG members disagree strongly with the students on this issue. Only 15% agree that this exclusion takes place.

8. Most principals felt they had relatively less influence over student dress regulations and student course choice.

9. John Geurnsey, "John Adams High School: Something for Everyone," in *High School*, ed. by Ronald Gross and Paul Osterman (New York: Simon and Schuster, 1971), pp. 263–71.

10. Often student governments will communicate their ideas to the SG adviser, who in turn will present the students' point of view to the principal. Principals appear to recognize the importance of the adviser's role since one of the criteria for effective student governments chosen by principals dealt with student governments' perceptions of the adviser.

11. It is interesting to note that the teachers in ESG schools do not have a higher level of morale than in other schools. However, neither are they less satisfied than other teachers. In other words, there appears to be no relationship whatsoever between teacher morale and either SG effectiveness or student morale.

4

Student Government as a Pedagogical Tool: What Do the Members Learn?

One clear finding from the preceding chapter is that the most dramatic differences between ESG and ISG schools occur in the responses of the SG members themselves. In this chapter, we consider in greater detail the consequences of involvement in student government for those students who are members. Whatever the broader effects of student government, effective or ineffective, on the student body as a whole, we would expect that those students who are SG members (always a small proportion of all the students in a school) would be affected by their experience.

Our problem is to determine what is learned by students who participate in student government. We take the view that curriculum consists of everything that occurs within the school from which students may learn something. Observers of the education process have often noted that many of the students' most important learning experiences are independent of the formal planned content of classroom instruction. They may learn from their school experience that various kinds of formal organizational structures are necessary to get things done or (a comment frequently made by free school students we have interviewed) that structures are inevitably oppressive and dehumanizing – that only a relatively anarchic "do your own thing" environment permits individuals to develop. They may learn that people can generally be depended upon or (as one student body president told us when asked what he had learned from his experience) that "you can't trust anyone." They may learn that they have no effective control over their own lives or that it is possible to change situations that are unsatisfactory.

We would argue that it is these attitudinal or "world view" learnings that are most likely to influence how students lead their lives after they leave school. We assume, then, that whatever other purposes student governments serve, they perform a teaching function as well. Whether or not this function is explicitly considered by school staff (and our strong impression is that it is rarely considered explicitly), students who participate in student government are bound to learn from their unique experience. We focus here on student government, not because we necessarily believe it to be the most efficacious mechanism for teaching decision-making skills and general attitudes about how collective decisions can be reached, but rather because it is currently the most common formal setting in Ontario's school system in which such skills and attitudes might be learned.

One direct method of obtaining information concerning the effects of an experience is to question the individuals involved. Thus, our first approach was simply to ask the several hundred SG members in our survey what they had learned – what effect their experience had had upon them. In the pages that follow, we note the overall responses and also, to complement the previous chapter, consider whether there are differences between ESG and ISG members.

The SG members were asked to agree or disagree with a series of statements describing five possible and frequently mentioned learning outcomes of their experience.

1. The first statement concerned decision-making: "Most students in this school would learn how to make better decisions if they served on student government." Just over 62% of the SG members agree. There is a small difference between effective and ineffective student governments that, surprisingly, favors ineffective governments (8% more ISG than ESG members agree with the statement). The same pattern of responses is obtained for the second, parallel, statement: "The longer I am involved in student government the more capable I am of making wise decisions." This negative relationship between SG effectiveness and learning of decision-making skills, though small, is most interesting. We noted in the conclusion of the previous chapter that the principals' criteria of SG effectiveness ignore a number of critical perceptions of students and teachers. It appears that one of the most critical areas overlooked by principals is the learning of decision-making skills. Schools are institutions whose job is pedagogical – they are supported from the public purse presumably because they provide opportunities for teaching and learning to take place. From this point of view, it is a sad commentary that fewer ESG than ISG members perceive themselves as learning what one would most expect people to learn from direct participation in government – how to make sound decisions.

2. It is often claimed that participation in student government activities should increase the students' appreciation of the value of democratic decision-making processes. We therefore asked SG members whether or not "my experience in student government has increased my appreciation of the value of the democratic process." Almost 60% agree. Since this is one of the criterion items used to classify student governments as effective or ineffective, responses from ESG members necessarily are substantially more positive than those from ISG members (80% of the former agree; 49% of the latter agree).

3. It is also frequently asserted that SG experience should increase the students' willingness and ability to accept responsibility. In response to the statement that "my experience in student government in this school has made me more willing to accept responsibility," just over two-thirds of the members agree. Here, there is a very large difference between effective and ineffective student governments: 92% of ESG members agree, while only 60% – 32% fewer – of ISG members agree. To the more pointed question, "If your school had an interesting project which needed a great deal of time and effort, could the school count on you for help?", 50% of ESG members said "definitely yes,"

while only 19% of ISG members so responded. When they were asked a question designed to tap their willingness to accept personal responsibility for decision-making in their later lives, however, there was no difference in the responses of ESG and ISG members.[1] It appears, then, that ESG members are more willing to assume the low-risk responsibility associated with implementing someone else's policies, but are not more willing to assume responsibility in higher-risk situations – situations where responsibility flows from authority, and where their decisions could have significant long-term effects upon their own lives.

4. Many authorities claim that experience in decision-making increases the students' sense of efficacy or control over their own lives – their sense that they can affect their own environment through direct action. When presented with the statement that "my experience in the student government of this school has increased my feelings of control over my own life," approximately 46% agree. But here again the responses from ESG members are much more positive (72% agree) than those from ISG members (39%).

Of course, ESG members know their way around the school. They are extraordinarily active in extracurricular activities and therefore probably know many students and teachers. They also seem to have an excellent rapport with the principal. Because much of their life centers on the school, increased feelings of control may be limited to the school environment.

Feelings of efficacy are valued in a democracy because individuals who possess such feelings are presumably capable of dealing with any organization, any bureaucracy, any government. In ideal type form, they are not cowed by the complexities of our large, impersonal organizations; instead, they will, with persistence and through responsibility, cut through the red tape, find the appropriate bureaucrat, and insist, with all likelihood of success, that justice be done.

In order to determine the degree to which ESG members have generalized their feelings of efficacy, they were asked whether they agreed or disagreed with the statement that "government decisions are like the weather: there is nothing ordinary people can do about them." Agreement with this statement indicates a low feeling of efficacy. Just under one-third (32%) of the ESG members agree, and almost one-half (45%) of the ISG members agree.

5. Finally, it is often suggested that SG experience should increase the students' desire to participate in voluntary groups outside school – to become participatory, active adults. When asked to respond to the statement that "because of my experience in the student government of this school, my desire has increased to become involved in such voluntary out-of-school groups as Pollution Probe, Ratepayers Associations, etc.," only 30% agree, and there is no difference between ESG and ISG members.

In three of these five direct outcome areas, more SG members responded positively than negatively, and on one other almost a majority (46%) responded positively. On two of the four,[2] the responses from ESG members were much more positive than the responses from ISG members. Interpretation of these data is, however, somewhat problematic.

One difficulty flows from the fact that SG members are not completely representative of the characteristics of students in general. There is a self-selection process that operates so that only certain types of students become interested in participating in student government. Moreover, many schools have rules that permit only certain classes of students to participate – the most common being a minimum required grade average. Thus, the responses of SG members to the questions noted above may reflect, not their SG experience, but their special qualities in relation to those of other students.

In order to determine just how different SG members are from students in general, we have compared the two groups in our sample on a number of characteristics. There are, first of all, no sex differences. The relative proportions of boys and girls among SG members are very close to the proportions in the total student population. There are also no important differences in the amount of time spent in working after school. The average student works 4.3 hours per week after school; the average SG member works 4.2 hours per week. SG members are on the average slightly older than students in general. The average age of students in the sample is 16.1 years and that of SG members, 16.6 years – a half-year's difference. Not surprisingly, then, SG members are also typically in a higher grade or year at school. Thirty percent of the students in general are in their fourth or fifth year in secondary school, as compared to 45% of the SG members. There is a slight tendency for SG members to come from more highly educated families. Among students in general, 20% come from homes where the father has received some postsecondary education, as compared to 26% of SG members. Conversely, 22% of SG members have fathers who received primary education or less, as compared to 30% of students in general. What is most surprising about this comparison is the relatively small difference, since it is often claimed that SG membership is heavily weighted toward the upper end of the social-class scale.

All of the differences noted above are small. There are, however, several areas where the differences are more substantial. First, with regard to parental educational aspirations, 51% of the parents of students in general want their children to attend university, as compared to 71% of the parents of SG members – a difference of 20%. Second, this large difference holds for students' personal educational aspirations as well: 42% of students in general and 62% of SG members would like to attend university. (These aspiration levels may be a better index of family social class than is father's education, since graduates of any level of the system may have widely varying occupations, incomes, and life styles.) Third, SG members also attain higher marks in school. In part, this fact reflects the minimum mark requirements often established for SG membership. Among students in general, 48% have an average mark above 70%; among SG members, 64% have attained marks in this range. Fourth, SG members are disproportionately in five-year rather than four-year programs. Sixty-six percent of students in general are in five-year programs, as compared to 83% of SG members. Finally, SG members are much more likely to participate in school activities other than student government. Fifty-four percent of students in general spend less than one hour a week in school clubs and other activities, while only

26% of SG members spend so little time in extracurricular activities.

Overall, then, there are a number of characteristics that sharply differentiate SG members from their fellow students. How should these differences be interpreted in relation to the learning consequences of participation in student government? In answering this question, two additional factors had to be considered. First, schools themselves differ considerably in the general opinions and attitudes students hold. What might be a very radical response in one school can be a relatively conservative response in another. Second, students in secondary schools are undergoing a process of rapid growth and change as a function of their growing older – changing from young teen-agers to full adults in the four to five years they spend in school. The effect of these factors must be taken into account in assessing the effects of SG participation.

The ideal approach would be conduct a longitudinal study: a group of students at the beginning of their SG experience would be matched with students not in student government, and the two groups would be observed over a long period of time. Within the time and budget allowed for this study, this type of analysis was not feasible. We therefore adopted, as an imperfect substitute, the following strategy.

For each SG member, we identified his school and year or grade in school. For each attitude or opinion variable used, we compared the response of the SG member with the average response of all students in his school and in the same grade, and assigned the difference as a score to the SG member. We then calculated the average difference score for all SG members in their first year in student government, for all in their second year, and so on, up to all those in their fifth year. By comparing each SG member only with students in his own school and grade or year, we controlled for differences between schools and between younger and older students. The assumption underlying the analysis was that, if students are indeed learning from their SG experience, the differences between them and the students with whom they are compared should increase with increasing years of SG experience; that is, they should become increasingly less like their peers.[3]

We first look at the effect of SG experience upon attitudes toward and satisfaction with the school itself. We asked all students and SG members how much satisfaction (on a four-point scale from "a lot" to "none") they got from various aspects of school life. In describing these results (and the rest that follow), we first note the overall response pattern among students and SG members, not taking into account school or grade or years of SG experience. We do so to give some idea of the point from which a trend among SG members grows. Then the trend among the difference scores is noted.

1. Satisfaction from athletics: 68% of students and 80% of SG members claim they get some or a lot of satisfaction from athletics. There is no significant trend among the difference scores year by year.
2. Satisfaction from participation in school clubs and activities: 49% of students and significantly more (66%) of SG members get some or a lot of satisfaction from clubs and activities. There is a small but steady trend for SG members to get increasingly more satisfaction with years of SG experience.

3. Satisfaction from relationships with teachers: 60% of students in general and 74% of SG members get some or a lot of satisfaction from relationships with teachers. Here, too, no trend is evident, indicating that the greater satisfaction has little to do with the effects of SG experience.
4. Satisfaction from relationships with administrators: 28% of students and 43% of SG members claim to get some or a lot of satisfaction here. There is very little increase in the difference between those SG members with one, two, or three years of experience, but a large increase after three years' experience. This situation indicates that, if the SG experience does have an effect here, it is only after several years of experience (and one must bear in mind the small number of subjects upon which four- and five-year experience is based).
5. Satisfaction from courses: 73% of students and 80% of SG members get some or a lot of satisfaction from their courses. An interesting trend occurs as a function of years of SG experience. SG members in their first year claim significantly greater satisfaction from courses than do students in general. This difference decreases among members in their second year. Among those with three years of experience, the difference changes from positive to negative, indicating that they are getting less satisfaction from courses than are their peers, and this negative difference then increases among those with four and five years of experience. It is interesting to speculate about what it is in the SG experience that causes members to become increasingly dissatisfied with their courses, relative to their peers, as they spend more time in student government.

Finally, in this area, we asked, "In general, how do *you* find life in this school?" The five possible responses were very boring, boring, ordinary, exciting, and very exciting. Twenty-three percent of students and 32% of SG members said life in school was exciting or very exciting. There is a slight tendency for the difference to increase with years of SG experience.

In general, then, SG experience has no effect upon satisfaction with athletics or relationships with teachers. It has a small but noticeable effect upon satisfaction with clubs and other activities in the school and with relationships with administrators, and upon a general feeling of excitement about school. The most dramatic impact is the increasing dissatisfaction from courses.

We next looked at the effect of SG experience upon members' feelings about and relationships with other individuals in the school. We first asked students and SG members whether they agreed or disagreed that "students in this school are passive" – one of the most common complaints heard from adults and students in the secondary schools. Fifty-five percent of students and 38% of SG members agree with the statement. Moreover, SG members tend increasingly to disagree, relative to other students, as their SG experience increases, indicating that they come more and more to see students as active. The difference changes, though, are not large.

We then asked the two groups whether they agreed or disagreed that "students in this school are treated like children." Equal proportions (29%) of students and SG members agree. Here, another interesting trend is evident. SG members in their first year disagree substantially more than do their peers. Members in their second year are much closer to their peers. After three years of experience, they agree more than do the students in general and after four years, the difference is even greater. Thus, SG members start out feeling less than do their peers that they are treated like children; but after several years of SG experience, their position is reversed. We suspect that this is not the kind of lesson that teachers and administrators want students to learn from participation in student government, but it appears to be the actual effect of this experience.

To get some additional information about student/administrator relationships, we asked students and SG members whether they agreed or disagreed with the statement that "in this school, there is at least one member of the administration (principal or vice-principal) who will listen to my opinions and views with respect and will treat me as an equal." Seventy-two percent of students and 78% of SG members agree. There is also a substantial increase in the difference after two years of SG experience. (It is interesting to compare these percentages with the responses to the question regarding degree of satisfaction from relationships with the administration: 28% of students and 43% of SG members reported getting some or a lot of satisfaction from such relationships. Apparently, the perception that some member of the administration treats one's views with respect and considers one an equal does not necessarily lead to a feeling of satisfaction from such relationships.)

We finally examined some generalized attitudes that are often claimed to be the product of experience in decision-making. It is suggested that decision-making experience increases the individual's willingness to place his trust in others – that he learns that people generally respond fairly and predictably. We asked both groups to agree or disagree with the statement that "most people in this world will take advantage of you if you are not careful." Agreement with the statement would indicate a lack of trust. Seventy-three percent of students agree, as compared to 67% of SG members. There is, however, a slight tendency for SG members to agree more than their peers as years of experience increases. It appears that SG members are initially only slightly more trusting of others than are their fellow students, but that they have a tendency to become more cynical as they gain experience.

It is also suggested that experience in decision-making should increase the individual's sense of control over his environment. He should learn that direct action can change circumstances and that by working hard at a problem, he can solve it. To tap this area, we asked both groups to agree or disagree with the statement that "to be a success in life, good luck is more important than hard work." Few students (8%) and fewer SG members (6%) agree with this statement. Moreover, no trend is evident with increasing years of SG experience.

Finally, one of the outcomes often claimed for SG experience is a greater belief in the responsiveness of political institutions – a feeling that such institutions can be made responsive to the will of the governed. We asked both students and SG members whether they agreed or disagreed that "government decisions are like the weather: there is nothing ordinary people can do about them." Fifty-one percent of students and 43% of SG members agree. Thus, SG members generally have only slightly more belief in the responsiveness of government. There is a fairly marked tendency for this difference to increase with years of experience, with an especially big jump between one and two years' experience. It may be concluded, then, that SG members start out slightly less pessimistic than their peers about government responsiveness and become even less so as time passes. This is the only area in which we have observed a significant "positive" learning from SG experience.

Looking over all of these results of these comparisons, what can we conclude? In most cases, the SG experience has no or almost no identifiable effect. In three of the four cases where some learning seems to be occurring – increasing dissatisfaction with courses, an increasing feeling that students are treated like children, and increasing cynicism regarding the trustworthiness of others – the lessons learned would be judged by most educators to be negative. In only one area – increasing belief in the responsiveness of government – could the lesson learned be judged as positive. Although the latter is only one area of learning, it is highly important to future citizenship behavior.

It may be the case that ESG members are learning more from their experience than are ISG members. We have been unable to test this proposition with these data, since, as noted above, the number of ESG and ISG members who had more than one year of experience would be too small to permit meaningful interpretation of their responses. This, then, must remain an open question, to be answered by future research.

Conclusion

To conclude, we should note again why we consider the question of how students learn to make decisions to be important. Many students in our secondary schools are over 18 years of age – they are legal adults. They can vote, they can drink, they can enter into legally binding contracts, and so on. They can make all of the decisions that independent adults are faced with. As soon as they leave secondary school, they are faced with the necessity of making decisions, more or less on their own. Young people, in and out of school, are indeed making many decisions, often not very good ones. Many are deciding to take drugs: drug convictions in Canada increased by 600% between 1965 and 1969. Many are deciding to have illegitimate children (or at least deciding not to do anything to prevent them): illegitimate birth rates increased by 30% between 1965 and 1969. In both cases the increases were especially notable among 15- to 19-year-olds. All over the province, students in grades 12 and 13 are deciding, in increasing numbers, to drop out of school, and so on.

We cannot stop young people from making decisions. But we seem unable to do much to teach many of them how to make good decisions, individually or collectively. They certainly do not learn how to make decisions in most formal classroom situations. They do not learn in school clubs and activities. They clearly are not learning much about decision-making from their SG experience and, of course, very few even have the opportunity for that experience. It would seem to us that we have here a substantial curriculum-building job (in the broad sense of curriculum) to which we have not yet given sufficient attention.

While principals often state that participation in student government is intended as a learning experience, in operational terms this statement usually means that students are provided with an opportunity to learn parliamentary procedure and to gain a modicum of experience in organizational and administrative skills. In recent years, there have been some schools and, in one case at least, a board of education and a private foundation that have sponsored leadership development sessions for SG members. These sessions are often designed to help students develop skills in group processes and interpersonal communications. What seems to be absent, however, are opportunities within most schools for students to develop decision-making skills by practicing under the supervision of trained personnel.

In his book *Helping Students Think and Value*,[4] Fraenkel cites Bloom's *Taxonomy of Educational Objectives* and lists the categories of the cognitive domain:

1. Knowledge: Knowledge simply involves the recalling of specific items of information.
2. Comprehension: Comprehension involves more than knowledge. For example, a person who comprehends something can not only recall it but can paraphrase it, review it, define it, or discuss it to some extent, also.
3. Application: The person who can use this thought process can do everything in categories (1) and (2) above. He can also demonstrate his ability to take information of an abstract nature and use it in concrete situations. It is this ability to apply information to new problems that makes the process unique.
4. Analysis: The essential ingredients of analysis include the breaking down of a communication into its constituent parts and revealing the relationships of those parts.
5. Synthesis: Synthesis is a word used to describe the process of pulling together many disorganized elements or parts so as to form a whole. It is the arranging, combining, and relating parts that makes this process unique.
6. Evaluation: Judgments about the value of materials or methods are evaluative judgments.

Much of the work in leadership development operates in the affective domain. These affective skills are, of course, an integral part of the decision-making process. Within the cognitive domain, schools stress knowledge and comprehension, and occasionally application. In some instances, analysis and synthesis constitute a small portion of the curriculum. Evaluation is the rarest component of school curricula.

As Fraenkel pointed out, the thought process required for evaluation – that is, choosing between alternatives or decision-making – requires many of the abilities of every other category, as well as some abilities unique to the evaluation category.[5] A principal who can involve his students in decision-making provides them with an opportunity to exercise more brain power, to utilize a greater range of cognitive and affective skills, than is applied to virtually any other segment of the curriculum.

Thus, real participation in decision-making, focused on issues that are sufficiently important to engage the serious attention of students, provides the opportunity to learn not only the skills directly associated with decision-making, but also some of the broader participatory values and attitudes mentioned throughout this book. Beyond these areas, participation in decision-making can provide for students one of the broadest and most comprehensive kinds of learning experiences that is available to them. It can be a very powerful pedagogical tool.

Many principals argue that SG members are not capable of understanding the implications of their decisions and therefore should not be involved seriously in decision-making. This view is like arguing that, because most students who begin first-year algebra are not capable of using the binomial theorem, they should not be allowed to enter the course. In pedagogy, we assume that students do not already know what is to be taught. We would argue that the only way for students to learn to recognize the implications of their decisions is through decision-making experience. Of course they will make mistakes. But we seriously doubt that many educators would wish to argue for other aspects of a curriculum that students should not have the opportunity to learn something if they are likely to make mistakes while learning. The problem — and it is by no means a simple one — is to view decision-making in the schools as a process of education. How do students learn to make more responsible decisions? How do they learn to make better decisions? We do not have ready answers to these questions. But unless a number of educators and students begin thinking about them, it is almost certain that we will never have the answers.

The evidence presented in this chapter suggests that SG members are not learning much from their experience. We should note, however, that students who participate in student government often learn the hardest lessons and, in their view, the most valuable ones when they work hard but accomplish very little. This comes out very clearly in the interview data and from the open comments of survey respondents.

One SG president, for example, is described by most of his SG colleagues as never changing or wanting to change anything "too far out of the way." The president happened to be in a school with a very authoritarian principal. By his own admission, the biggest accomplishments of his year as president were to raise with the principal the ideas of phasing out the student adviser and eliminating parliamentary procedure from SG meetings. Both ideas were vetoed by the principal. While, in his words, he got "nothing but opposition from the principal" and he viewed the student body as "apathetic," he informed us that he had learned a great deal and was glad he had had the opportunity to serve as president. He explained his learning experience as follows:

I had been in a fantasy world believing that all people are basically nice. I've learned the hard way that people are not naturally nice. Some kids have treated me like mud. I guess this is what the cut-throat business world is like. Well, I learned to be friends with some people and to praise certain people. I also learned not to let people bother you and that most are easy to impress.

This quote provides a good indication of what many SG members may learn: the belief that people are basically nice is part of a fantasy world. It is this cynicism that many SG members take as part of learning to make "better" decisions. Cynicism — the contemptuous distrust of human nature and motives — seems almost endemic to student governments. In schools that rank highest in SG effectiveness, over 50% of the SG members agree with the statement that "most people in this world will take advantage of you if you are not careful." In all other schools, 60% to 75% of SG members agree. Moreover, as we noted above, SG members tend to agree more with this statement as they spend more time in student government. It was Henry Lewis Stimson who said: "The only way to make a man trustworthy is to trust him; and the surest way to make him untrustworthy is to distrust him and show your distrust."[6]

One grade 10 girl was just beginning to cross the thin line beyond which she would translate her principal's unwillingness to give responsibility to the student government into a belief that he mistrusted it. In a voice that almost pleaded, she told us:

If there's a majority vote in student council then Mr. W. [the principal] should go along with it. We're representatives of the students and most students would agree with us. So he should let us have a trial period and see how it works out. You know, try out hot pants or open dances. And, if anything happened we would be responsible for it. Just to see what it would be like to have all the responsibility.

Stimson also said: "The only deadly sin I know is cynicism."[7] Unfortunately, cynicism seems to be one of the few identifiable outcomes of their experience for SG members in Ontario's secondary schools.

Notes

1. The statement presented to students was "I would prefer to have a job where I could decide how to do most things myself." Approximately 80% of the SG members agree or strongly agree and approximately one-third strongly agree, regardless of the effectiveness of their student government.

2. Number 2 is not included in this summary statement, since it is an effectiveness item and differences between effective and ineffective student governments exist by definition.

3. The questions used for this analysis are not the same as those used to assess directly SG members' impressions of what they had learned, since those questions are applicable only to SG members. Also, the analysis does not compare effective with ineffective student governments. This comparison would have been valuable, but unfortunately it would have so reduced the number of students with more than one year's experience for both groups as to make the entire analysis meaningless. There were 499 SG members with one year of experience, 154 with two years, 58 with three years, 22 with four years, and 4 with five years. Since very few of the respondents had four or five years of experience, the results of the analysis can be considered reliable only for comparisons of individuals with one, two, or three years.

4. Jack R. Fraenkel, *Helping Students Think and Value* (Englewood Cliffs, N.J.: Prentice-Hall, 1973), p. 30.

5. *Ibid.*

6. Henry Lewis Stimson, cited in *Familiar Quotations* by John Bartlett (Boston: Little, Brown, 1955), p. 839.

7. *Ibid.*

5

The House System

Chapter 3 led to the conclusion that student governments in general, as they exist in Ontario, do not seem very successful in accomplishing their own goals, those set for them by principals, or generally accepted citizenship goals. When one finds differences at all, they are only between extreme cases, and even then they are substantial only among SG members themselves. Further, on the basis of the detailed analysis in Chapter 4, the possible pedagogical outcomes of being an SG member are either negative or not realized at all.

In this chapter, we examine in some detail an alternate organization structure for student participation that has gained some popularity in Ontario secondary schools – the house system. If traditional forms of SG organization are not accomplishing their goals, perhaps this new organizational form could be more successful.

The house system takes a variety of forms, but they all involve the division of the entire student population of a school into several units (usually four) called houses. Each student is associated with one unit – one house – in the hope that he can more easily identify with the smaller unit than with the entire school. Through his house, a student is encouraged to become involved in a variety of activities and events. Presumably,

a well-organized house system provides a framework for social interaction and competition and gives students an opportunity to belong to a smaller "school" within the school. Given a supportive set of conditions, students will compete with fellow students to gain recognition for their house in academic, athletic, club and service or administrative activities.[1]

Although the house system has only recently gained popularity in Ontario, it is a relatively old school organizational form that has long been common among private schools, including the famous public schools of England.

In most cases, the house system forms the basis for an SG organization. For example, SG representatives are typically elected by and from the various houses within a school. It is notable that Ontario schools with a house system typically have a larger proportion of the student body directly involved in student government than do schools without a house system.

The house system is worth careful consideration not only because it is the most prominent new organizational form in Ontario secondary schools for promoting student participation in school life, but also because a number of advantages have been claimed for adopting it in Ontario secondary schools. Specifically, in a recent article by King and Warren,[2] the house system was proposed as a solution to many of the problems alleged to have been generated by the adoption of the credit system with individualized student timetables in the province. Given that the King-Warren article is the most thoroughgoing and widely known advocacy of the house system, their arguments are used as an organizing framework for the first part of this chapter, and the data generated in our study are applied to them to determine whether a house system does indeed have the advantages claimed for it. In the latter part of the chapter, we consider some other possible consequences of adopting a house system that go beyond the scope of the King and Warren thesis.

Of the schools in our random sample, 15 have a house system and 20 do not (in 3 additional cases, the information provided was insufficient to determine whether or not a house system existed). Understandably, larger schools are more likely than smaller schools to have adopted a house system, although the principal of one school with only 300 students reported that he had instituted one. Of the 21 schools with enrollment over 1,000, 11 have a house system (52%), while only 4 of the 14 schools with fewer than 1,000 students have one (28.6%). To evaluate the King and Warren arguments, comparisons are made between large and small schools with a house system (HS) and without a house system (NHS).

The King and Warren Arguments

King and Warren present a series of interrelated arguments, all of which deal with negative consequences of the credit system.[3] They maintain that the system has such immediate effects as isolating individual students and such long-range consequences as increasing the dropout rate and increasing the risk of producing a generation of "alienated young people, with a narrow, confined social outlook."[4] They also suggest that individualizing programs may:

1. Reduce the teaching of abstract educational values
2. Increase a student's feeling of being segmented
3. Diminish a student's ties with his school
4. Decrease the amount of student participation in extracurricular activities
5. Reduce students' opportunities for discussing with teachers such topics as personal aspirations.[5]

They then propose that one way to avoid or correct these problems is the adoption of a house system.

However valid or invalid the King and Warren arguments may turn out to be, it is clear that they have tapped a line of thought that is quite popular among secondary school administrators in Ontario. As part of a follow-up study on the house system, telephone interviews were conducted with the individuals in charge of the house system in each of the 15 HS schools in the sample. These individuals were asked, among other things, why they had implemented a house system. In six of the 15 cases, they specifically mentioned problems created by the introduction of the credit system. In another six cases, although the credit system was not specifically mentioned, problems of "identity loss" among students were cited. In only three instances was neither of these factors part of the justification.

With this background, we turn to the specific arguments advanced by King and Warren.

Position I: Extracurricular Activities
The first argument runs as follows:
1. Under individual timetabling, a "student spends each period with a different combination of students."
2. This situation results in transitory relationships, "leaving little opportunity for the development of solid friendships" or "stable social relationships."
3. The absence of solid friendships results in students' feeling more isolated than they did under the home-room system.
   From these assertions, King and Warren conclude that
4. This isolation increases the risk of cultivating "a mass of alienated young people, with a narrow, confined social outlook."

We have no data with which to test directly any of these premises. The conclusion regarding alienation is considered below (position IV). King and Warren, however, use the isolation assumption (4) in conjunction with another to generate a conclusion that is tested here. They argue that the absence of stable social relationships – a condition of social isolation – diminishes student participation in extracurricular activities. This diminishment occurs because, before a student will engage in such activities, he needs a great deal of social support. "Students are not inclined to participate in school activities alone, and it is necessary to provide a supportive network of social relationships in order to encourage them to do so."

By establishing a house system, it should be possible to provide the support necessary to encourage students to participate. The first hypothesis derived from the King-Warren argument is *HS schools have a greater percentage of students participating in extracurricular activities.* This expected differential in participation is presumed to result from a lack of social support available to students in NHS schools.

The second hypothesis derived from their argument is, *A greater percentage of students in NHS schools than in HS schools explain their lack of participation by the absence of friends in the extracurricular activities that most interest them.* King and Warren quote a student as saying that house systems "need more variety in what would appeal to non-athletic people." Athletic activities are generally available in most schools. Therefore, if there are marginal increases in participation, or if the house system appeals to more of the different types of students (that is, to non-athletic types), then one can also hypothesize that, *HS schools have a different pattern of participation.*

Several different pieces of information can be brought to bear upon the first hypothesis – namely, that the percentage of students who participate in extracurricular activities is greater in HS schools. Students were asked whether they were members of or participated in any of the following types of school clubs or activities: musical groups, debate and/or dramatics, publication groups, subject matter clubs, hobby clubs, prefect society, athletic teams (competing with other schools), athletic teams (intramural), social committees, or other groups.

Students were also asked to indicate if their school did not have a particular type of club or activity. Participation rates (percentages of students who claimed membership or participation in an existing activity) were then calculated for each type of club or activity among students in large and small HS and NHS schools.

Among large schools, NHS schools have slightly higher participation rates (from 1% to 7% higher) in every activity but one – hobby clubs – and there the rates are the same (10% of students in NHS schools and HS schools claim membership in such clubs). Among small schools, participation rates in NHS schools are slightly greater than in HS schools in all but three areas – hobby clubs (where the rates are 11% for both HS and NHS schools), prefect societies (2.9% participating in NHS schools as compared to 5.4% in HS schools), and intramural athletics (45% participating in NHS schools as compared to 49.1% in HS schools). The data, then, fail to support the hypothesis.

This evidence, however, is not conclusive. In some schools, one may have a few students participating in many different activities, while equally high (or low) participation rates in various activities may result from many students participating in fewer activities. Consequently, we calculated for each school classification the percentage of students participating in at least one club or activity. The results are rather striking. Among large schools, 62% of the students in HS schools participate in at least one extracurricular activity, while 73% of students in NHS schools are participants, a difference of 11%. In small schools, 67% participate in HS schools and 76% participate in NHS schools, a 9% difference. Thus, in both large and small schools, the percentage of students who participate in at least one activity is greater in NHS schools.

It could, of course, be argued that although fewer students in HS schools participate, those who do participate in such schools do so more actively – that is, they spend more of their time in extracurricular activities than do participants in NHS schools. Students were asked in the questionnaire: "About how many hours per week do you *usually* spend in school clubs, activities or teams?" The responses of those who claimed to participate in at least one activity were tabulated for each school type. Looking first at a fairly low level of participation, in large NHS schools, 60% participate more than one hour per week, as compared to 58% in large HS schools – really no difference. Among small schools, the difference is greater (64% versus 56%) but still favors NHS schools. At a higher level of activity, for the percentage that spends more than three hours per week in school activities, the results are similar; that is, there are higher percentages in NHS schools. This is also the case for a very high level of participation, the percentage that spends more than 10 hours weekly in extracurricular activities. To put the matter another way, the average amount of time spent per week in extracurricular activities by participating students in HS schools is 2 hours and 20 minutes. In NHS schools, the corresponding figure is 2 hours and 42 minutes, almost half an hour more.

Is it then the case, as the second derived hypothesis suggests, that those in NHS schools who do not participate are more likely to cite lack of friends in activities as the reason for their non-participation? Students were asked to indicate which of six reasons best explained why they did not take part more in school activities. The alternative responses were:
1. I already spend a lot of my time in school activities
2. I have to work after school
3. It would be hard to get a ride home
4. I don't have any friends in other activities
5. I've got better things to do
6. Other.

The responses among non-participating students in the four school types were compared. The salient response for our purpose is number 4, "I don't have any friends in other activities." More non-participants in NHS schools do cite the absence of friends as their reason for not participating in extracurricular activities, the difference being greater among small schools (1.5% in HS schools as compared to 6.1% in NHS schools). In no school, however, is this a popular reason for lack of participation, for in no case do more than 8% of the non-participants cite it. Thus, although the second hypothesis is formally supported by our data, it is a weak form of support, since lack of friends in other activities is a very uncommon reason for non-participation in all types of schools. On the basis of the available data, we simply cannot claim that substantial numbers of students in NHS schools refrain from participating because of a lack of friends in the activities of their choice.

We turn, then, to the third hypothesis, namely, that one would expect to find substantially different patterns of participation in HS and NHS schools and, in particular, higher participation in non-athletic activities in HS schools. To test this hypothesis, the pattern of memberships[6] across the 10 types of clubs and activities specified earlier was calculated for each of the four school types. Looking first at the gross distinction between athletic and non-athletic memberships, we find little difference among large schools (47% of memberships are in non-athletic activities in HS schools and 48% in NHS schools). Among small schools, we find a substantial difference, favoring NHS schools: 40% of memberships are non-athletic in small HS schools, while 50% are non-athletic memberships in small NHS schools. It seems, then, that a house system does not generate higher levels of participation in non-athletic activities.

Examination of the data on an activity-by-activity basis shows that small differences are evident. A participant from a large HS school is somewhat more likely to engage in hobby groups and intramural sports than is a student in a large NHS school (7.5% as compared to 6.3% for hobby clubs and 28.0% versus 25.4% for intramural athletics). Among small schools, much the same pattern obtains, but participants from small HS schools are also more likely to be involved in prefect societies (3.6% as compared to 1.5%) and interscholastic athletics (27.7% as compared to 25.7%). Even in these areas where differences exist, however, they are very small and cannot, by any stretch of the imagination, be said to constitute substantially different patterns.

Position II: The Segmented Student

King and Warren's second argument suggests that:

1. A student operating under an individualized timetable is assessed in different ways by different teachers according to the subjects he is taking. "For example, he can be seen as serious in a class he finds challenging but as disinterested in a class in which he feels insecure."
2. This differential perception means students play multiple roles, "being one person to one teacher and a different person to another."
3. These multiple roles create a feeling of segmentation and a subsequent need to close this void – "to feel that at least someone in the vast bureaucracy thinks of them as a whole person."

From this, King and Warren conclude that "it may be that this lack of continuing teacher/student contact and stable social environment has contributed to the increasing dropout rate."

The first point to be made about this argument is that it is logically faulty as an attack upon the credit system. Even in the old lockstep group programming days, students took different classes with different teachers, with the consequent need (or opportunity) to play multiple roles during a school day, to be a different person in different classes. Their argument holds as a support for the house system only if it is true that the house system encourages or creates generally closer teacher/student relationships. Thus, the first hypothesis to be derived from the King-Warren argument is, *Student/teacher relationships are closer in HS schools than in NHS schools*. A second hypothesis relates directly to the conclusion of the argument, *Dropout rates are lower in HS schools than in NHS schools*.

Regarding the first hypothesis, we note that if a house system has the ameliorative characteristics claimed for it, then more students in HS schools than in NHS schools should develop deeper rapport with more teachers. Teachers in HS schools should be much more likely to view students as "whole persons." Students should find more teachers who listen to their views and opinions with genuine interest, more teachers who treat them as equals, and more teachers with whom they can discuss personal problems, than do their peers in NHS schools. Several pieces of information can be brought to bear on these questions.

Students were asked, "How many teachers do you know in this school who listen to your views and opinions with genuine interest?" The alternative responses were none, one, a few, many, most, all. Among large schools, a house system does not seem to affect the responses: 11.6% of the students in HS schools have yet to find even one such teacher, as compared to 9.9% of the students in NHS schools. The most typical response in both sets of schools is about the same: just over half the students claim to know a few teachers who demonstrate genuine interest.

In the smaller schools, the differences are more noticeable, though still not large. Those that do emerge, however, favor NHS schools. Almost twice as many students in small HS schools claim they do not know a single teacher who listens to their views and opinions with genuine interest (15.6% as compared to 7.9% for NHS schools).

Students were also asked, "How many teachers do you know in this school who treat you as an equal?" Again, the response choices were none, one, a few, many, most, all. In large schools, there are not any substantial differences between HS and NHS schools. In no response category is the difference greater than 1%. As before, slight differences among small schools favor NHS schools. For example, among small HS schools, 72.6% of students claim to know more than one teacher who treat them as equals, and the corresponding figure for NHS schools is 78.9%.

The third question put to students was, "How many teachers do you know in this school with whom you could discuss personal problems?" The pattern of responses in the four sets of schools remains the same: there are no significant differences between the large schools and slight differences between the smaller schools favoring those NHS schools. For example, 36.6% of students in HS small schools claim they know at least a few teachers with whom they could discuss personal problems, as compared to 40.2% of students in NHS schools. What is perhaps most interesting about the responses to this question is the extraordinarily large percentage of students who say they know no teachers with whom they could discuss personal problems. In the HS schools, large and small, about 43.5% of the students make this claim, while in the NHS schools 41.3% of the students say there is not a single teacher with whom they could discuss a personal problem.

A comparison of the responses to these three questions suggests that the feeling among many students is that there are at least some teachers who listen to their opinions with genuine interest and who treat them as equals. Their feelings do not, however, carry over to the view that teachers can be approached for help with personal problems. In any case, there is no evidence that a deepening in student/teacher interpersonal relationships takes place automatically as a result of implementing a house system.

Is it the case, then, that dropout rates are lower in HS schools, as the second derived hypothesis suggests? The most direct manner of testing this argument would be to look at dropout rates in HS and NHS schools. We did not collect data on the dropout rates, and the information that is available from other sources is incomplete and may not be reliable. We did, however, ask students how they would feel if they had to quit school. The possible responses were:

1. Very happy – I'd like to quit
2. I wouldn't care one way or the other
3. I would be disappointed
4. I'd try hard to continue
5. I would do almost anything to stay in school.

If the respondents who say "very happy" or "wouldn't care" are the most likely to drop out, then there are small differences that favor NHS schools. Among large HS schools, 18.7% of the students choose one of these two responses, as compared to 16.1% in NHS schools. Among small schools, the difference is slightly greater and in the same direction: 19.7% in HS schools as compared to 13.6% in NHS schools. Looking at the other end of the scale, at the students who are most committed to school (who answer that they would do almost anything to stay in school), we again find that NHS schools have more holding power: 19.3% of students in large NHS schools choose this response, as opposed to 13.0% in large HS schools. Among small schools, the figures are, respectively, 20.7% and 15.1%.

Position III: School Ties

King and Warren combine their argument concerning the social isolation of the student with shifts in responsibility for course selection and conclude that, under individualized programming, there is a diminishing of ties with the school. Their argument is as follows:

1. Students now "have the major responsibility of determining the majority of courses that make up their program throughout their high school career."
2. They are, however, "seldom provided with opportunities to discuss personal aspirations, their lack of success in certain courses, and the implications of taking one course rather than another."
3. "This shift in responsibility for course selection, often compounded by a sense of isolation, tends to diminish a student's ties with his school."

Turning first to the second point, the authors do not suggest how a house system would increase the opportunities for students to discuss with teachers such matters as the implications of course choice. Indeed, the evidence just presented indicates that such opportunities do not necessarily arise as a result of the house system. There are, however, other relevant data from our survey that throw light on the question.

We asked students how many of the credits they were taking were decided upon after consultation with their parents *and* a member of the school staff (that is, a teacher, guidance counselor, vice-principal, or principal). If a house system is designed to provide more opportunities for student/staff discussion around such concerns as course choice, then a greater percentage of students in HS schools could be expected to have discussed their choice with the school staff. But this is simply not the case. In all types of schools, regardless of size or the presence or absence of a house system, about 55% of the students did not discuss course selection with both their parents and a member of staff.

The concluding point in the King-Warren argument is that the shift in responsibility for course selection, coupled with the sense of isolation students develop as a consequence of individualized programs, tend "to diminish a student's ties with his school." The diminishing of ties may be reflected in ways other than a decrease in participation, such as an increase of boredom and feelings of reduced involvement in the school.

To test the feeling states of students we asked them how exciting or boring they find life in their school. About one in five students finds his life in school very exciting or pretty exciting, and close to one in four finds it pretty boring or very boring. About half the students find themselves feeling indifferent, perceiving schools as neither exciting nor boring but simply ordinary. Students' responses apparently are not related to the size of their school or to the absence or presence of a house system (25.5% of students in all NHS schools find life boring or very boring; 26.0% of students in HS schools feel this way; 24.1%

of students in NHS schools find life exciting or very exciting; 22.1% of students in HS schools share that feeling).

Students were then asked how involved they feel in what goes on in the school (very, fairly, or not at all involved). Here, too, we find very small differences. In large HS schools, 41.9% of students claim they are not involved at all, compared to 40.2% in large NHS schools. Among small schools, the corresponding figures are, respectively, 34.5% and 32.7%. At the opposite extreme, for students who feel very involved in their school, HS schools also do slightly less well. In large HS schools, 4.9% of students choose this response, while 7.6% of students in large NHS schools feel very involved. Among small schools, the difference is greater but in the same direction: 9.4% in HS schools as compared to 13.3% in NHS schools. In no case, however, can it be said that large percentages of students feel very involved in the life of their school. Among all students in the sample, only 7.9% choose the very involved response.

Finally, to solicit students' opinions about how other students felt about life in school, we asked them whether they agreed or disagreed that "students in this school are passive." Slightly more students in HS schools than in NHS schools agree (57.8% versus 54.2%). Teachers also were asked this question, and their responses parallel the student opinions (64.6% of teachers in HS schools agree; 60.0% in NHS schools agree).

If these data on feelings of involvement, boredom, and passivity are valid indices, students' ties with their school appear to be very tenuous. Moreover, adoption of a house system does not appear to be strengthening them.

Position IV: Alienation and the Lack of Abstract Educational Values
Perhaps King and Warren's two most serious criticisms of the credit system with individualized programs revolve around their long-run consequences. The first argument, already outlined under position I, concludes that there is a risk that the system will cultivate "a mass of alienated young people, with a narrow, confined social outlook." The second argument suggests that individual timetabling takes more of the teachers' time and, as a result, abstract educational values such as selflessness and a sense of commitment are not taught.

Once again, it is suggested that a house system minimizes these consequences, presumably by increasing the level of social integration of the school. We have already presented evidence that level of social integration is not necessarily associated with the presence of a house system. Moreover, as teachers in HS schools spend more time on house organizational and administrative problems, it might be expected that they would have less time, rather than more, to teach abstract educational values. It may be, however, that such values are best learned by example, and teachers who demonstrate a sense of commitment to house activities do more to modify students' value systems than teachers engaged in moral education courses.

The question of what kind of evidence bears upon the level of alienation in a school is a difficult one, for it is an extraordinarily complex concept. One of the best treatments of the subject is found in a recent paper by Anderson, in which alienation is defined as consisting of five separate dimensions:[7]

1. Powerlessness: A low expectancy of ability to determine outcomes or reinforcements sought in the school.
2. Meaninglessness: A low expectancy of ability to make satisfactory predictions about the future outcomes of behavior in the school.
3. Misfeasance: An expectation that the use of means which are prohibited by school authorities is necessary in order to attain goals desired by the student.
4. Futility: Assignment of low reward values to goals and beliefs that are highly valued by school authorities.
5. Self-estrangement: Participation in school and school-related activities based largely upon anticipation of future rewards rather than upon rewards inherent in participation, such as pleasure or satisfaction.

Regarding two of these dimensions — meaninglessness and futility — we have no evidence. We do have some evidence relating to the other three.

We first consider powerlessness. As defined by Anderson, powerlessness refers to the sense that an individual cannot influence the actions and decisions of others that affect him. In Chapter 2, we discussed at some length the responses to a series of questions designed to assess the perceptions of students (and other groups) about the amount of influence exerted by various individuals and groups on a variety of school decisions. It will be recalled that each student was asked to rate the influence of each group or individual over each decision area on a four-point scale, ranging from none (1) to a lot (4). As part of this exercise, students were asked to rate the influence of "students in general" and "you yourself." To measure individual powerlessness for each student, the difference between these two ratings was calculated for each of 10 decision areas, and then averaged across them. This figure provides, then, a measure of the student's perception of his own personal influence relative to that of other students in his school.

We felt it important to measure this dimension in relation to an individual student's feelings about the influence of students in general in his school, since a student's perception of how much influence he *should* have would normally be affected by his perception of how much other students usually have. A student with little personal influence in a school where he perceives students in general as having little influence might not feel himself to be particularly powerless. Conversely, a student with substantial personal influence in a school where he perceives his fellow students as having more influence might think of himself as being relatively powerless. That is, the norms against which students judge and react to their own situation are a function of their perception of the situation of their peers.

A positive score on this index means that a student sees himself as more influential — more powerful — than his peers. A negative score means that a student sees himself as less powerful. The higher the positive or negative score, the relatively more powerful or powerless a student perceives himself to be. The average levels of this index among students in the four school types were calculated.

Although students generally see themselves as more influential than students in general (all the averages are positive), those in NHS schools feel themselves more powerful, by a substantial margin, than do those in HS schools, in both large and small schools (large HS schools, 0.158; large NHS schools, 0.221; small HS schools, 0.074; small NHS schools, 0.160). Along this dimension, then, we cannot say that students in HS schools feel less alienated.

The second alienation dimension for which we have measures is misfeasance. One of the most popular prohibited means of getting a message through to school authorities is vandalism. More important than actual acts of vandalism (which can vary from school to school with such factors as the opportunities available, the amount of policing, and the location of the school) are student attitudes toward such acts – their willingness to condone an extreme form of prohibited behavior.

To test students' attitudes toward vandalism, we asked them to state how they would feel if they observed someone committing an act of vandalism on school property. Large HS schools have a slightly lower percentage of students who would be sorry to see such an act occur (78.6%, as compared to 83.3% in large NHS schools). The greatest differential in responses, however, comes from the small schools, where 91% of the students in NHS schools say they would feel sorry as compared to only 71% of the students in HS schools. At the other extreme, among students who would be glad to see an act of vandalism, there is essentially no difference in large schools (3.3% of students in HS schools and 2.7% in NHS schools claim they would be glad or very glad to see such an act). The difference is slightly greater in small schools, where 7.2% in HS schools but only 1.4% in NHS schools indicate a supportive attitude toward vandalism. These data suggest a somewhat higher level of alienation in HS schools.

As we indicated in Chapter 1, an increasingly popular non-legitimate means of expressing discontent is through student protest. If students in HS schools were less alienated, we would expect to find fewer of them expressing support for protests than in NHS schools. The reverse is the case. In large and small HS schools, 77.4% of reporting students expressed support for the most recent protest in their school. In NHS schools, about 8% fewer (69.1%) supported the most recent protest.

A willingness to condone vandalism (or indeed be happy about it) or to support protest activities suggests the absence of a relatively concrete value commitment to the school. In order to assess students' attitudes toward their school along this commitment dimension, we asked, "If your school had an interesting project which needed a great deal of time and effort, could the school count on you for help?"

The responses from large HS and NHS schools are almost identical. There is a difference, however, in the small schools, and it is logically consistent with the students' expressed views on vandalism. Almost twice as many students in small NHS schools were willing to express a strong commitment to their schools (22.1% as compared to 11.8% answered the question "definitely yes").

The third alienation dimension to which our data apply is self-estrangement. The salient question here is whether students in HS schools get more satisfaction from their school activities than do those in NHS schools. Students were asked how much satisfaction they got from courses, from clubs and other extracurricular activities, and from athletic activities (with answers on a four-point scale: a lot, some, very little, or none).

We first consider the percentages of students in HS and NHS schools who claim to get some or a lot of satisfaction from courses. There is no difference among large schools (77% in HS and in NHS schools), and a slight difference in small schools in favor of NHS schools (79% versus 81%).

Next, we examine the percentages of participating students who get some or a lot of satisfaction from their participation in extracurricular activities (excluding athletics). Among large schools there is a small difference in favor of NHS schools (38% as compared to 35%). Among small schools there is a substantial difference favoring HS schools (44% versus 32%). It will, however, be recalled that the evidence we brought to bear upon the first King-Warren argument demonstrated that, among small schools, participation rates were noticeably smaller among students in HS schools than in NHS schools. It can be concluded, then, that in small HS schools (compared to small NHS schools) fewer students participate in extracurricular activities, and spend less time in those activities, but more of them get satisfaction from their participation.

Finally, we consider the percentages of students who get some or a lot of satisfaction from athletic activities in the various types of schools. Although the differences are small, they do favor slightly NHS schools – to a very small degree large schools (70% as compared to 72%) and somewhat more substantially small schools (73% as compared to 79%).

Teachers were also asked whether they thought most students in their schools were satisfied or dissatisfied with school. The results are striking. In NHS schools (large or small), just over one-third of the teachers think most students are dissatisfied (34.8%). In HS schools, almost one-half (49.4%) feel most students are dissatisfied.

What can we conclude, then, regarding the fourth King-Warren position? On two dimensions of alienation, our data do not support the notion that alienation is lower in HS schools. On the third dimension, self-estrangement, the evidence, with one exception, favors NHS schools. We therefore must take the position that the available evidence does not generally support the King-Warren argument.[8]

Some Broader Attitudes

Up to this point, we have focused upon conditions within the school, upon how students feel about and behave in the school environment in which they spend many hours per day throughout the year. But as we noted in Chapter 1, one of the main reasons for being concerned with questions of student participation in school governance is that what students learn in and about their school presumably affects how they act as citizens after they leave school. Thus, although these particular questions are not dealt with by King and Warren, we should consider how students feel about the wider world around them. Specifically, what attitudes toward other people, and toward government in general, are they developing while in school? If the house system has the advantages claimed for it, then presumably students in HS schools develop more positive attitudes toward other people and government in general than do students in NHS schools.

The students in our sample were presented with a few questions designed to tap these broader attitudes. To assess their attitude toward other people, we asked them whether they agreed or disagreed that "most people in this world will take advantage of you if you are not careful." Agreement with this statement indicates a rather pessimistic view of other people, of a sort not supportive of free participation in joint decision-making processes. In NHS schools, 71.2% of students agree. In HS schools, 75.9% agree. Students in HS schools are slightly more pessimistic about the kind of behavior they can expect from other people. What is most striking is the high proportion of agreement: just under three-quarters of all students in the sample feel that other people cannot be trusted. This is hardly a testimony to the effectiveness of schools as teaching grounds for democratic living.

In order to test student attitudes toward government in general, we presented them with the following statements and asked them to agree or disagree: (1) "Government decisions are like the weather: there is nothing that ordinary people can do about them;" (2) "The government of this country is doing its best to find out what ordinary people want." Students in HS schools are somewhat more likely than their peers in NHS schools to agree with the first statement (52.6% as compared to 49.9%). They are also more likely to agree with the second statement (44.9% as compared to 42.8%). Thus, students in HS schools have a slight tendency (compared to students in NHS schools) to believe that although they cannot do much about government decisions, these decisions nonetheless take into account the concerns of ordinary people. We would suggest that a person holding these two views sees government as a sort of benevolent dictatorship: it tries to act in his best interest, but there is little he can do to affect it. If a house system has any influence at all on student attitudes toward government (and the differences are small), it seems to be in the direction of perceiving government as a benevolent dictatorship. This is hardly an attitude set likely to help students to function effectively in an increasingly participatory society.

Implementation of the House System – A Possible Counterargument
The data presented in this chapter have failed to support any of the arguments advanced by King and Warren concerning the ameliorative effects of the house system. It could, of course, be argued that our data are irrelevant for purposes of analyzing the effectiveness of HS schools. King and Warren did inform their readers that "the staff of some schools do not understand the raison d'être of such systems and are introducing them in a token way." They could simply argue that the schools we have analyzed as HS schools do not reflect effective systems. This, however, is a dangerous argument. If it is held that none of the schools in our sample went beyond tokenism, one might well question the feasibility of trying to introduce an organizational form that is so difficult to implement.

An alternate argument would be that only a few of the schools in our sample represented a fully implemented house system, but that these were insufficient in number to influence the overall response patterns from HS schools. This would be an especially telling argument if a house system was typically instituted in schools that experienced serious difficulties with student life and participation. Under these circumstances, the few effective schools might raise the overall HS scores to a level closer to the NHS average. Given the increasing popularity of the house system, we decided to try to test this argument.

The first problem was to develop an index of HS implementation. We consulted Dr. King and Ms. Warren, since they had carried out a very detailed study of a few schools that apparently had a fully implemented house system. On the basis of their experience, they suggested that we ask the following questions of each HS school:

1. Do you have a house system coordinator?
    (a) If yes, does the coordinator receive extra pay and/or a reduced teaching load (excluding spare duties)?
2. Do you have house masters (teachers or administrative guidance counselor)?
3. Do your house masters (teachers) receive extra pay and/or a reduced teaching load?
4. Is your house system organized primarily for intramural athletics?
    (a) If yes, by the physical education department?
5. Does your house system include and award points for the following activities:
    (a) Intramural athletics
    (b) Intercollegiate sports
    (c) School clubs
    (d) Administrative and organizational tasks (leadership and organizational; referees, score-keepers)
    (e) Academic achievement?
6. (a) Is your student council integrated with the house system executive?
    (b) Does your house system executive take the place of a student council?
7. Does each house meet together as a group more than once during the year?
8. Are points in the competition among houses awarded for:
    (a) Winning
    (b) Participation?
9. Are your home rooms composed of students from the same house who stay together throughout their high school careers?
10. Have you made some attempt to locate each house in a specific part of the school?
11. Do all the teachers belong to a house?

To form an index, the number of "yes" responses were counted. The higher the score, the greater the implementation of the house system.

Telephone interviews were then conducted with an official from each of the HS schools in the sample, the implementation scores were calculated, and the schools were divided into three groups: high implementation schools (scores of 12 to 16 out of a possible total of 16); medium implementation schools (scores of 7 to 11); and low implementation schools (scores of 0 to 6).[9] The responses of students on each of the questions referred to in the first analysis of the King and Warren arguments were then calculated for each level of HS effectiveness, and compared with each other and with the responses from NHS schools. The

King and Warren arguments would be supported if either or both of two response patterns were discovered for each item: (1) the outcomes from high implementation HS schools were more positive than the outcomes from NHS schools; and/or (2) there was a clear increase in a positive direction in the outcomes from low to medium to high implementation schools.

In only three of the more than 20 items considered was one of these patterns revealed by student responses. The first concerns the percentage of students who do not participate in other activities because they have no friends in them: 4.8% of all students in NHS schools choose this response. Among low, medium, and high implementation HS schools, the percentages choosing this response are, respectively, 8.6%, 3.1%, and 4.2%. Thus, although the high effectiveness figure differs little from the NHS figure, the high implementation response is more positive than the response from low implementation HS schools. The difference is slight, and the absolute percentages are small, but the trend is in the right direction.

The other two areas that support the King-Warren hypotheses relate to the degree of student satisfaction from non-athletic extracurricular activities and from athletics. In both cases, the differences are small but they are in the appropriate direction to support the King and Warren argument regarding alienation. It must, however, be recalled that one of these (non-athletic activities) was one of the few areas where the original data analysis, as reported above, supported the pro-HS position.

Thus, there are only two cases where this supplementary analysis of student responses provides *additional* support for the King and Warren arguments, and in both cases the support is only marginal. We conclude that examination of the attitudes and behavior of students does not support the position that introducing a house system will make a noticeable positive difference in secondary schools in Ontario.

Student Government Member Responses

The reader may recall that, when we considered SG effectiveness in Chapter 3, we discovered that the differences between schools with effective and ineffective student governments were important only among SG members themselves. With this fact in mind, we carried out this same supplementary analysis on the responses of SG members in low, medium, and high implementation HS schools. Here, the results are quite different. In 10 cases (almost half of the questions considered originally), the SG member responses follow a pattern supportive of the King and Warren arguments. The SG member responses from NHS schools and from low, medium, and high implementation HS schools for these 10 questions are presented in table 13. In most cases, the differences are not large; and in three cases, the pattern among HS schools is curvilinear, with the best scores coming from medium implementation schools and the next best response from high implementation schools. Nonetheless, there does appear to be a significant pattern among these responses suggesting that a house system does have some effect upon SG members.

Since only a very small percentage of students in a school is ever an SG

Table 13/Responses of Student Government Members in Schools With and Without a House System to Questions Supporting the King-Warren House System Argument

Item	NHS Schools	HS Schools (by degree of implementation) Low	Medium	High
Average number of hours per week spent in extracurricular activities	4.2	4.0	4.4	4.9
% who do not participate more in extracurricular activities because of lack of friends in other activities	1.7	3.1	1.9	1.0
% who claim that many, most, or all teachers listen to their views and opinions with interest	37.7	31.5	38.6	52.2
% who claim many, most, or all teachers treat them as an equal	35.0	31.3	35.1	37.0
% who would be very happy or happy to leave school	10.2	15.3	8.6	6.4
% who say that life in school is exciting or very exciting	31.5	27.0	34.5	39.8
% who are not at all involved in their school	14.1	11.7	3.5	8.3
% who would not care or would be glad if they saw an act of vandalism	8.8	10.6	8.6	3.7
% who say the school could not count on them for help in an interesting project	13.7	15.3	3.5	6.4
% who get some or a lot of satisfaction from athletic activities	76.5	74.4	76.8	80.2

member, this evidence does not provide strong support for the establishment of a house system. It might, of course, be argued that these data are significant; that because the house system is a new form of organization in most schools, there has been time for only those most directly involved in school governance, the SG members, to be affected by it. One could then expect the influence to spread out slowly to the rest of the student body. This argument does not hold, however, for the house system is not so new a phenomenon that only a few centrally involved students could be expected to have been affected by it. Among the high implementation schools, one had had a house system for only one year when the questionnaires were completed, two for three years, and three for five years. Thus, the average length of experience with a house system among these schools was 3.7 years. Among the medium effectiveness schools, one had had a house system for one year, two for four years, and one for six years, for an average length of experience of 3.7 years – identical to the high effectiveness schools. Among the low effectiveness schools, one had had a house system for two years, one for three years, one for four years, and two for six years, producing an average length of experience with a house system of 4.2 years, the highest of the three groups. Of the 15 HS schools included in this analysis, only three had operated a house system for fewer than three years at the time of the study, and nine had their system in operation for four years or more – a time sufficient for almost an entire cohort of students to have passed through the school. It is likely, then, that the great majority of these schools had their house system long enough for some effects outside the student government to have been observed if they were ever going to occur.

Conclusion

We must conclude that a house system, even if very effectively implemented, does not much affect the attitudes and behavior of students in the school. If teachers or principals are truly interested in developing a better atmosphere in their school or helping students to become effective participants in school life and the adult political community, it would not appear to be particularly profitable to invest a large amount of time and energy in instituting a house system. The payoff simply is not very great. Educators might better spend their time and energy trying to devise innovations that will have some more noticeable positive effect.

Of course, we have little evidence that a house system is detrimental. If it does little good, it does not appear to do any harm. In some cases, a house system may be useful in a small way – for example, as a means of organizing and administering intramural athletics. One secondary school principal, after reading a preliminary version of this chapter, commented, "If only one student who previously felt isolated is able to make a few friends through a house system, then it is worth the effort." This may well be a sound argument, provided that the cost of instituting and operating the system is not large. If a substantial amount of work is required, however, the data presented here indicate that establishing the system would be counterproductive, for the school staff would be losing the opportunity to adopt another approach that might be more productive.

Notes

1. A. J. C. King and W. K. Warren, "House Systems: Problems and Perspectives," *Orbit*, III (December, 1972), 4.

2. *Ibid.*, pp. 4–7.

3. From reading the article by King and Warren, one might conclude that the authors strongly oppose the credit system. However, this is not the case. As Warren states: "We never intended to denounce the credit system and a glance at Dr. King's previous reports, *The School in Transition* [Toronto: Ontario Institute for Studies in Education, 1970] and *Innovative Secondary Schools* [Toronto: Ontario Institute for Studies in Education, 1972], would attest to this" (personal correspondence, February 28, 1974).

4. All quotations in the following pages are from King and Warren, pp. 4–7, unless otherwise indicated.

5. All of this assumes that in pre-credit system days students felt less segmented, they had stronger ties with their schools, they participated more heavily in extracurricular activities, and they had more ample opportunities to discuss personal questions with their teachers – debatable propositions!

6. A student belonging only to a subject matter club would count as one membership in that club; a student participating in four different activities would count as four memberships, one in each of the activities.

7. Barry D. Anderson, "School Bureaucratization and Alienation from High School," *Sociology of Education*, XLVI (Summer, 1973), 316–17.

8. These results parallel the results of other studies of the credit system carried out in OISE concurrently with this study. In these studies, there is no evidence that a great deal of alienation has been created by the credit system. The final results of these other studies were not available when our data were being analyzed; but it can now be noted that even if the house system was quite successful in other respects, there is not a large amount of alienation in Ontario secondary schools for it to counteract. See W. G. Fleming, *The Individualized System: Findings from Five Studies* (Toronto: Ontario Institute for Studies in Education, 1974), pp. 61–62.

9. Six schools were rated as high, four as medium, and five as low on implementation of of their house system.

6

Summary, Conclusions, and Recommendations

In this final chapter, we briefly summarize the need for and current state of student participation in decision-making in Ontario's secondary schools, and identify some of the factors that we believe to be major blocks inhibiting the development of student decision-making skills.

The Need for Student Participation in Decision-Making

According to the 1968 Report of the Provincial Committee on the Aims and Objectives of Education in the Schools of Ontario (the Hall-Dennis report), there is only one official publication of the Ministry of Education that "deals with the aims [of education] deliberately and fully"[1] – a publication known as the Ontario Programme of Studies.[2] The Hall-Dennis report summarizes the Programme of Studies as advocating "a society in which the individual has opportunities for self-realization, security and participating in decision-making."[3] The program, then, is the only official Ministry document that explicitly specifies student participation in decision-making as an aim of education.

There are two significant facts about the Ontario Programme of Studies. First, it was published in 1937. As the Hall-Dennis report notes, "it suffered a major set-back on this continent during and after World War II, partly because of the continuing war or cold war mentality and inability or reluctance to recruit or educate teachers for anything more than forceful instruction in facts and skills."[4] It might be added that, as far as the practice of student participation in decision-making is concerned, the "set-back" has yet to be eliminated.

The second fact about this document is that it applied only to grades 1 to 6. So, according to the only Ministry ruling statement in this area, if you are a student beyond grade 6, you have missed your opportunity to participate in decision-making.

In Circular H.S.1, the document that gave Ontario the credit system, the Ministry of Education carefully avoided providing an explicit policy statement concerning the participation of secondary school students in decision-making. Instead, a descriptive statement was provided: "Seeking an opportunity to relate more deeply to the individual student and to involve the student more actively in student decision-making, principals and teachers alike are changing traditional curricular and organizational patterns."[5] Thus, although there is no official policy statement prescribing student participation in decision-making in Ontario secondary schools, there is recognition that many teachers and principals hold this as a goal. In addition, as we have indicated, some high-ranking officials at the board of education level have gone on public record as favoring such participation.

Several reasons for developing effective mechanisms to permit student participation in high school decision-making have been advanced throughout this book. These can be summarized as follows:

1. It is perhaps an unfortunate commentary on the state of our education system that the most common reason for increasing student participation in decision-making cited by high-level education officials is that such participation will help to curb student unrest. Rarely are "educational qua educational" justifications heard. Nonetheless, increased participation may well help to remove many of the sources of student protest in the secondary schools.
2. From the "fact" of student protests comes a second and related argument. Many argue that students already have power, as evidenced by the number and outcomes of student protests. To these individuals, the choice is not whether students should or should not have power – they already have it. The choice is among the various options available for exercising that power.
3. Styles of participation in the political life of Canadian society are changing, especially in the large urban areas where most Canadians live. No longer is one's duty as a citizen discharged solely by casting a ballot at periodic intervals. Rather, citizens are actively seeking involvement and taking a part in the resolution of issues that directly affect their lives. This involvement requires individuals who are skilled and experienced in the art of individual and collective decision-making. It also requires citizens with a high sense of political efficacy, who feel that governments can be changed and that they and other citizens have the power to influence political decisions. As Byron G. Massialas noted:

> The political orientations that children develop, largely determine the political culture that will prevail. Cultures in which there is a relatively high degree of citizen involvement (civic cultures) are generally comprised of people who view themselves as politically efficacious. That is, they feel that they can, through their own efforts, influence political decision-making. Nations in which people have very little concern for changing the government through their own efforts tend to have parochial political cultures; in these nations the citizen expects virtually nothing from the political system. Systems that provide open mechanisms for rapid change and are responsive to the demands of their citizens, appear, in historical perspective, to have more chances for political survival and continuity than those systems that have no institutionalized means of change.[6]

Recent evidence suggests that a great deal of learning about how the political system works, and their own place in it, occurs among students during their secondary school years.[7] That secondary students are developing political orientations that will eventually determine the nature of our political system seems clear. The question is, what are they learning?

4. The changing legal status of adolescents imposes increasing rights and responsibilities on young people. To deal with the options that are now available to them, it is imperative that students develop evaluative and decision-making skills while they are still in school. One cannot wait until they are in the labor market and hope that somehow things will work out.
5. Contemporary educators tend to focus statements of educational objectives upon the development of the "whole" child, stressing both cognitive and affective development. Collective decision-making and decision-making for conflict resolution are necessarily relevant to the affective as well as the cognitive domain.
6. Educators have long held that one of their major jobs is to "teach students to think." According to experts in the field, rational decision-making is the highest stage of cognitive development.
7. The final reason for concern with teaching students how to make decisions, which in a sense incorporates many of the points noted above, is that young people living in a technological society such as ours will lead successful lives (a situation that is, after all, the ultimate objective of all socializing efforts, including schooling) only if they can thread their way through an incredible array of choices available to them. It is a peculiar condition of modern life that one's fate is not as fixed by inherited cultural norms or the station in life of one's parents as it was in previous eras and still is in many simpler societies. As Maurice Gibbons noted:

> The major challenge for young people in our society is making decisions. In primitive society, there are few choices; in technological societies like ours there is a bewildering array of alternatives in life-style, work, politics, possessions, recreation, dress and relationships, environment and so on. Success in our lives depends upon the ability to make appropriate choices. Yet, in most schools, students make few decisions of any importance and receive no training in decision-making or in the implementation and reassessment cycle which constitutes the basic growth pattern. Too often, graduation cuts them loose to muddle through for themselves. . . . The test of life is not what he [the student] can do under a teacher's direction but, what the teacher has enabled him to decide and to do on his own.[8]

Simply put, if we do not provide young people with the opportunity to learn how to make decisions in a complex and changing world, we are failing to equip them with the one skill that, more than any other, we can predict they will need in order to live successfully in the kind of society we will leave to them.

What Are the Schools Doing to Teach Decision-Making Skills?

In the preceding chapters of this book, we considered the effectiveness of the two most common school structures in Ontario, which have as one of their objectives the encouragement of student participation in decision-making: (1) the student government, found in almost all Ontario secondary schools; and (2) the house system, found in a large and increasing number of schools. Neither appears to be doing the job at all well. The only positive effects observed were on SG members themselves, who always represent a small proportion of the total student body of a school. Moreover, as we indicated in Chapter 4, most of the differences between SG members and other students seem to be less a result of their SG experience than of the initial differences in background and attitudes between SG members and other students.

Where else in school might students learn decision-making skills and attitudes? Teaching good citizenship has long been an avowed goal of Canadian Studies courses, especially civics classes. We did not specifically investigate these, however, since little seems to have changed since 1968, when *What Culture? What Heritage?* was published. This book was a condemning indictment of what passes for effective citizenship training in school classes in Canada. The following quotations tell the dismal story:

Most of us would agree that the ability to weigh and evaluate evidence, to think critically and independently, to read with discrimination, to form opinions based on facts and knowledge, to express ideas clearly and so on are highly desirable attributes in the citizens of a democratic society. With the pace of change so rapid and the increase in knowledge so great, it is probable that they are more important in the long run than any factual information learned in school. Most of us also would agree that these goals can be partly achieved in the history or social studies classroom. . . . And yet, in our entire Survey we saw only 127 classes (15 percent of the total) that were consciously designed to encourage, by deliberate procedures, the development of mental abilities beyond the minimal learning skills inherent in most lessons.[9]

Are students learning anything from their civics classes? The answer seems to parallel the data in our study: a significant outcome is indifference or cynicism. "Our evidence suggests that . . . the strongest, most widely held attitude of the students in our Survey was either complete indifference or deep cynicism toward politicians and political life."[10]

Why does this situation exist? Note the following description of most civics classes in Canada:

What young Canadians learn about the structure and functioning of their government is . . . outmoded. Civics classes continue to concentrate on an old-fashioned, purely descriptive account of the three levels of government, with very little analysis or realism. The psychological or sociological motives for voting, the influence of the mass media, the roles of political parties, the effects of lobbying and pressure groups, the decision-making processes, the importance of bureaucracies, power elites and other factors that bring politics to life seldom get into the Canadian studies classroom. The cynicism of many of our young people toward politics is caused partly by the unrealistic oversimplified courses of study in civics.[11]

That this pervading cynicism about government and the ways of influencing it continues to exist in our secondary schools is borne out by many of the responses of students to the question in our own survey, administered five years after *What Culture? What Heritage?* was published. Seventy-three percent of the students believe that "most people in this world will take advantage of you if you are not careful." Just over half (51%) believe that "government decisions are like the weather: there is nothing that ordinary people can do about them." Less than half (45%) believe that "the government of this country cares a lot about what ordinary people think of new laws." Regarding their own school government, the form of government that is closest to their own concerns, almost two-thirds (64%) believe that "student government in this school is just a tool of the administration." Less than half (49%) believe that "SG members are keeping other students informed about important questions that are being discussed." Eighty-one percent believe that "the teachers and principal do not let students who strongly disagree with them run for student government in this school." Only a third (36%) believe that "the SG members are the true leaders of the students in this school," and less than a third (31%) believe that "the SG members represent the best political skills among the students in this school."

Secondary school students in Ontario, then, have neither learned very much about decision-making nor acquired usefully positive attitudes about government in general. All of the blame for this situation cannot, of course, be placed upon the school. Young people learn much outside school. But if the schools are not solely responsible for the creation of the unfortunate outcomes we have discussed here and elsewhere in this book, clearly they are doing little to counteract the outside influences, to alter the negative learnings students are acquiring.

This is not to say nothing can be done – that the situation is inevitably hopeless. One does occasionally find demanding, exciting, and productive formal Canadian Studies classes. What is done by some teachers can presumably be done by others, although the changes in behavior will not come easily. One also does occasionally find schools where students have been given real authority to make important decisions and have learned much from the opportunity. Perhaps the most poignant example turned up during one of our case studies of a free school. Students who came to the school had "learned" from their "straight school" experience that any form of structure and formal decision-making process is oppressive. Over the course of a year of struggling with real decisions – arranging courses, hiring teachers, dealing with disruptive behavior, and so on – they came to realize that some sort of formal process was necessary for converting a vague feeling of consensus into a decision that could be acted upon. Then they realized that, although this procedure was necessary, they did not know how to do it. This may be a small step, but it is the indispensable first step for long-lasting learning to take place – to realize both that one does not know something and that it is important to one's life to learn it. Of course, it is not easy to give students real decision-making authority, so that they may first learn that they need to know how to make decisions and subsequently learn the process for making them. It entails some risks. They may make bad decisions or silly decisions or (what can be worst of all in some cases) no decisions at all. But we suspect that the risks involved are smaller than most teachers and principals believe.

We note, as an example, the experience of many schools in Metropolitan Toronto when, in the fall of 1973, teachers undertook a work-to-rule campaign as a negotiating strategy with the boards of education. Among other things, this situation meant that teachers were not available to serve as coaches or advisers for the great variety of extracurricular activities found in most schools. The expectation was, of course, that all of these activities would cease to function without teacher support. But in many schools the students themselves organized and ran the activities. Athletic teams were coached by older players; concerts and plays were organized and produced by the students; in cases where adult presence was legally required, 18-year-old students (who are legal adults in Ontario) were pressed into service in this role, and so on. We have no solid evidence as to how widespread this phenomenon was; but personal observation, combined with reports from other observers and students themselves, suggest that it was surprisingly common. Moreover, no disasters appear to have resulted from it. Students were left to their own devices, placed in a situation where they had to make all the important decisions regarding their own activities; and generally, they did a competent and in many cases an excellent job. We were most impressed by the conversations we had with students who were involved in running their own activities during this time. We observed a unique sense of excitement, of accomplishment, of pride in their achievements; and most importantly, we found students describing what they had learned about decision-making – where and why they had made mistakes, what they had had to do to correct them, how they would do things differently, what options they would select next time, what good decisions they had made, and why and how they had come to make them.

It appears to us, then, that this is one area where some relatively simple steps can be taken toward meeting the pedagogical aims of student participation in decision-making that have been advanced in this book. Students should be given considerably more authority over the various extracurricular activities in which they participate (it should be noted that of all the students in our survey sample, approximately 70% claimed to participate in at least one extracurricular activity, as compared to the very small percentage of students who have the opportunity to participate in student government).

Some ancillary evidence from our survey can be brought to bear on this suggestion. The reader will recall that we asked students who claimed membership in various clubs and activities in their school to indicate whether adult advisers or students "control most things" in the activity. We compared the responses to a number of the other questions that reflect desirable outcomes from our point of view, of students who saw adults as controlling things and students who saw students as controlling things. Those who perceive students as having control are less likely to believe that "most people in this world will take advantage of you if you are not careful," are less likely to believe that "government decisions are like the weather," are less likely to find school boring, are more likely to feel involved in school life, and are more likely to claim to get some or a lot of satisfaction from their participation in these extracurricular activities. The differences are consistent in the sense that those who see students as controlling most things give more positive responses, but they are in no case large. It must be remembered, however, that in most schools the activities of extracurricular groups are highly regulated and constrained by the administration or by the student government, which most students see as a "tool of the administration." Thus, the number of things that either an adult adviser or students can control is typically quite limited – a far more restrictive situation than many of those that we described as developing during the Toronto work-to-rule campaign. Yet, even under these restricted circumstances, some degree of positive outcome is associated with student control.

Permitting students to have much greater formal decision-making power in their extracurricular activities, then, appears to be a useful and relatively simple step that can be taken. We do not see it as a substitute for the much more difficult job of permitting students to participate more fully in the making of general school policies, whether through the student government or some other mechanism; or for the task of improving the quality of instruction in formal civics classes; or as a substitute for reorienting our thinking toward making training in decision-making a central aspect of a total school curriculum. It may, however, be an important first step.

The Role of the Principal
Obviously, if any of our suggestions are to be effectively implemented, it must be recognized that the principal plays a key role. If authority is to be shared, it is to a large extent the principal's own authority that is involved. As Dan W. Dodson noted: "If I were betting on any of the potential solutions of the social problems of the high school, I would put my money on the principal."[12]

Principals, like other members of society, are divided in their views concerning student participation in decision-making. Many define all students' efforts at participation in decision-making as necessarily leading to what mathematical game theorists call "two person zero-sum games"[13] and what Kenneth Fish prefers to call "distributive conflict situations."[14] These are games or situations of conflict in which one person's gain is the other person's loss. This is a rather tragic definition for a principal to hold: it means that the principal's "win" is the students' "loss" and vice versa. More significantly, it means that the principal's win signifies society's loss – that the principal and society do not share an identity of interest – for, as we have argued throughout, society needs individuals who are efficacious and possess organizational and decision-making skills.

Kenneth Fish, an experienced high school principal, pointed out that a number of conflict situations arise in secondary schools that are not of this zero-sum type but are better portrayed as "integrative conflict situations" or *non*-zero-sum games, that is, conflict situations where "if each team or party to the conflict competes intelligently, each will win more."[15] There are, for example, principals who define students' requests for a curriculum committee as a distributive conflict situation: if the students win the right to have such a committee, the principal loses. But, as Fish pointed out, such a committee takes nothing away from those in power. Rather, it is likely to increase greatly the total pool of ideas.

There are many situations that appear at first glance to be distributive conflict situations but that can, with some creative effort, be transformed into an integrative conflict situation. Ontario students place smoking lounges high on their list of priorities. One principal we interviewed has consistently refused student requests for a smoking lounge and has refused in a manner that students perceive as arbitrary and dogmatic. The principal has never informed his students of his reason, which is (as he explained to us) that smoking endangers health and he does not want to contribute to this health hazard. Students – even SG members – are not aware of his feelings. It is quite likely that a student council, familiar with the evidence that relates smoking and cancer, would agree with the principal's goal to minimize the number of students who smoke. But this principal, by his constant, unexplained refusal, has missed the opportunity to determine whether or not an identity of interest exists between the student government and himself. Consequently, he has also missed the opportunity of gaining insights into the motivation of students to smoke and of finding possible solutions to the problem. At the same time, he has increased the students' feelings of alienation.

In another school, a principal accepted the idea of a student smoking lounge on the grounds that he could not, in good faith, permit teachers to smoke while denying the right to students. He told his student government that it could operate its own lounge with the proviso that, if the furniture got burned or torn up, he would close the lounge. After one month, he inspected the premises. As he expected, the furniture was badly damaged, and the lounge was closed. The SG members felt that the principal had acted in good faith and that he was a wise predictor. They are now considering offering student funds to pay for the damaged furniture and are trying to figure out a way to reopen the lounge and prevent the furniture from being destroyed again. These students are actively involved in a problem-solving task. They are attempting to find a creative solution to a problem – a problem that they now view as their own and of their own making, primarily because the principal gave the problem to the students rather than "protecting" them from it. In this case, the principal defined the smoking lounge issue so that he and his student council shared an identity of interest.

We are not suggesting that all conflict situations can be redefined into integrative conflicts. There are times when principals have to deal with distributive conflict situations; and doing so, of course, means that either the principal wins and the students lose, or vice versa. But by gaining experience and developing better interpersonal relations through integrative conflicts, the parties, when involved in distributive conflict, are better able to accept a compromise or a loss without having the loss destroy the relationship.

The case cited above, of the principal who turned the smoking lounge problem into an integrative conflict situation from which both parties gained, is not unique. An increasing number of principals shares the views reported in the Canadian Education Association's survey of secondary school principals, *Man in the Middle*:

Our students run their own show except for the money. If our board would care to take over any deficits incurred by students, I would turn this over to them. At the moment, because our students are minors, I keep a pretty close check on finances because I am legally responsible.

Students should be involved to the point that they are aware of the motivation behind school policy. Most adolescents are sensible, alert and intelligent and, if a policy cannot be sold to a large percentage of them, then the policy is doomed to failure.

Both teachers and students grow as they participate in meaningful decisions.[16]

Any principal who nowadays doesn't allow teachers and students to have a part in policy-making, won't last long as a principal. The question is not whether they *should* have a share or not but, how *much* of a share.[17]

As a principal in our own survey noted:

If students feel that they are treated as human beings by the principal and the teachers, then they are not too concerned about looking for reasons to protest. Walk-outs, sit-ins, picketing, etc., simply are means to annoy a school in return for annoyance caused by teachers and principal.

But even principals who share these views, who want to involve students in decision-making as part of a general pedagogical strategy, face a number of problems. It is to these that we now turn our attention.

Some Obstacles to be Overcome
Location of Authority Outside the School
In many boards, the principal lacks authority over a large class of decisions that are crucial for increasing student participation; and in some cases, these decisions are totally outside the authority of any officials directly responsible for the education process. For example, during the course of this study, we interviewed a principal from a school in Metropolitan Toronto. The principal had in his office a scale model of an innovative recreation area designed by students in one of their classes. The land for which the park was designed was adjacent to and owned by the school. The principal was excited by and proud of the design and the model. We asked him if the students were interested in implementing their design. He told us that they were eager to do so and that he and his staff also were enthusiastic. It was necessary, however, to get permission from the Building and Plant Department.[18] When the principal sought such permission, he was informed that students could not work on the project. He was not entirely sure of the reason behind the refusal. He thought it might have had something to do with students not understanding the safety regulations or, perhaps, union objections to having non-unionized labor work on the project. When we asked him if he had technical teachers who knew or could understand municipal building regulations, he assured us that he did. When asked what evidence he had that unions would object, he admitted he had none.[19] Several weeks after the interview, one of the authors happened to be at a meeting with a former high-level employee of the Building and Plant Department. When this individual was asked to explain the position of the department, he replied that principals could easily exploit students by forcing them to do manual labor within the school. "Someone has to protect these kids from being exploited."

It seems to us highly unlikely that students in Ontario are exploited or that there is much chance of their being exploited by school principals coercing them into manual labor. But even if such a risk does exist, the Building and Plant Department is clearly not the proper location for final authority over a decision concerning a student project designed in the classroom. This is an educational decision and should be considered by authorities concerned with and knowledgeable about the education process, not by authorities who operate a service agency. The principal felt that he had lost a valuable opportunity to provide a positive educational experience for a group to increase their feelings of involvement in the school. The opportunity was lost because the decision-making structure of his school system is poorly designed – a structure for which the board must assume ultimate responsibility.

The Reward System for Principals

School principals often are viewed as working within a reward structure that militates against change. Particularly to be avoided is any change that might place the school and the principal in the center of public controversy. As one trustee told us, "a principal who rocks the ship simply doesn't get ahead . . . and rocking the ship includes creating any kind of problem in which his supervisors must take a hand." One principal told us that, for his colleagues and himself, a crisis is defined as "five telephone calls from parents, all complaining about the same thing." We have also noted that most school officials who support student participation in decision-making justify their position on the grounds that student involvement constitutes a major strategy for curbing student unrest. While this may or may not be a valid argument, the fact remains that it is the one that school officials assume carries the most weight with principals.

Student unrest presents a real problem to principals who are intent on maintaining a "low profile." It can generate a great deal of publicity, which in turn can create serious controversy about school policies – policies for which the principal is responsible. No principal likes to be placed in a position where members of the general public or the news media accuse him of failing to exercise control over the school. And while there are some principals who believe that their board officials will support them, there are others who believe exactly the opposite. Trustees also are not relied on for support. A Canadian Education Association monograph reported that "most high school principals believe that most board officials have a fairly sympathetic understanding of the principal's job (though they believe most trustees do not)."[20]

Principals who promote student participation in decision-making do so at a risk. On the one hand, there is the belief (or hope) that student participation will decrease the probability of student protest – a desirable end from the principal's perspective. On the other hand, there is the possibility that permitting students to share decision-making might lead to open conflict between some community members and the principal. For example, if students have complete control over a dance and some students get drunk or arrested for taking drugs, predictably some good citizen will publicly accuse the principal of abdicating his responsibility. It also is possible that some trustees will side with the irate parents (who did, after all, elect them); they may even be sufficiently influential to persuade, coerce, or otherwise manipulate some senior board officials to side with parents and urge that the principal be transferred to a different (and less desirable) school.

But what of the principal who believes that there is no possibility of student unrest in his school? If he has a non-supportive board, then involving students in decision-making means that he is taking a substantial risk. A successful experience is not rewarded to the degree that an unsuccessful experience is punished. *Control* is a key word in educational circles. Perhaps the most frequent "educational topic" among teachers is how to maintain classroom discipline. One of the most humiliating experiences for a teacher is to have a student misbehave while the principal is observing; and one of the most frequent complaints by teachers who view themselves as "liberated" is the feeling that the principal or vice-principal insists on teachers maintaining relative quiet in the classroom. The *Schools Administration Act* of Ontario defines, quite explicitly, the duty of the teacher "to maintain proper order and discipline in his classroom and on the playground"; the first duty of the principal is to "maintain order and discipline in the school."[21]

The maintenance of order is a norm into which new teachers are rapidly socialized. This norm, coupled with the reward and punishment structure of the school system, helps to explain why many principals, even those who would like to, are reluctant to provide students with opportunities to participate in decision-making.

Lack of a Curriculum on Decision-Making
A third difficulty faced by principals who wish to increase students' skills in decision-making is the absence of research-based curricular guidelines and material. For example, no one in Ontario has systematically examined elementary classroom situations at different grade levels in order to determine whether a student, as he increases in age, is provided with the opportunity to make increasingly complex decisions. Informal interviews with teachers, principals, and parents of students in elementary schools suggest that a coordinated strategy is not even considered. Yet most educators agree that, as children mature, they should be given more responsibility. If it is the case that children do have increased opportunities to participate in decision-making within the classroom as they increase in age – and this is doubtful – these opportunities clearly do not occur in any planned and coordinated fashion.

The Hall-Dennis report stressed the idea that the curriculum is not confined to the classroom but consists of all activities that take place within the school. This conceptualization of curriculum is necessary if one is to design a set of learning experiences for students that will provide them with the opportunity to learn increasingly complex decision-making skills as they mature.

Interpersonal Relations
As we have indicated, principals are faced with a number of problems, many of which are structural or systemic. In addition, there are affective problems that inhibit the development of situations in which students learn decision-making skills.

One of us recently led a workshop for the Ontario Secondary School Union. During the course of the discussions, the group began to focus on students' attitudes toward SG members. One student made the rather surprising statement that he and most of his friends were afraid to make suggestions or enter into discussions with the student government. When asked why, he gave two reasons: first, the SG members in his school constituted an elite group and therefore were not easily approachable; second, the opportunity to ask questions or to offer suggestions was limited to assemblies and SG meetings. He had made suggestions at a few of these gatherings and, in his words, had been "put down by the student council president." He found this a very humiliating experience, which taught him to fear the power of the student government.

A second student volunteered a similar story. By the time the discussion ended, it became clear that a large percentage of the non-SG members in the group had identical feelings – they were simply afraid of their student government.

While conducting one of the case studies, we interviewed various SG members concerning their relationship with the principal. Many of them agreed that one positive point about him was that he required them to think through any suggestions they made and present their position, often in writing, in a clear and logical manner. Later in the conversation, they told us of some of the suggestions that he had rejected. When we asked about his reasons for rejecting them, they said they did not know and had never asked. It gradually emerged that the students were afraid that, if they asked the principal for an explanation, he would view them as insolent and "get angry at them for questioning his authority."

Fear, then, is a major characteristic of these relationships. SG members are often afraid of the principal, and students are often afraid of their SG representatives. As noted earlier, the strongest formal role that student governments play is to operate in an advisory capacity. To fulfill this function effectively requires an openness of communication, both between students and their representatives and between the principal and the student government.

Any individual who has entered a group with a strong fear of someone in that group knows how inhibiting this feeling can be. Typically, when a person feels his fear, he responds to it and, in so doing, is unable to be fully receptive to the ideas of others. Further, intense fear of someone in the group reduces a person's spontaneity, creativity, and openness. Trust cannot begin to grow until fear has been acknowledged, dealt with, and properly disposed of.

But fear, as a characteristic of interpersonal role relationships in the school, is not confined to the students' fear of their representatives or the representatives' fear of the potential wrath of the principal. Parents often complain about something a teacher did or said to their child but do not discuss the matter with the teacher. When asked why they have not spoken to the teacher about the problem, they admit that they are afraid to do so, afraid that the teacher will be angry at being criticized and retaliate by punishing the child.

Teachers often have related stories of children in their classes who appear to have severe problems. When asked if the behavior was reported to the parent, many say it was not. Subsequently, it turns out that the teacher is afraid that the parent will interpret his report as a criticism of the parent's child-rearing ability and respond with a vengeful anger.[22]

There is, then, something in the process of schooling that appears to create fear of others in the context of the school. Some suggest that this is the consequence of an institutional commitment to order and discipline – a value commitment that necessarily drives schools toward a punitive orientation. Parental fear is explained as a response to their own early experience of schools. Others argue that fear is the result of a school authority structure that provides the principal with a degree of power over school affairs that is perceived by those within the school as dictatorial but with no formal accountability to the teachers, parents, or students.

Conclusion

In the preceding pages, we noted a number of obstacles that must be removed in order to increase the involvement of students in decision-making and consequently increase the probability that they will learn those attitudes and skills regarding decision-making that seem essential to their successful functioning as members of our society. A common theme running through this chapter is fear – in particular, the fear of others' power. We have noted that the reward system for a principal operates so that he often has much to fear from significantly increasing student participation in decision-making. Moreover, SG members often fear the principal, students often fear the power of SG members to humiliate them, and mutual fears frequently underlie relationships between parents and teachers.

We suggest that this fear-permeated atmosphere is at the root of many of the problems we have discussed. It is well known that fear is a powerful inhibitor of innovative (which usually means risk-taking) behavior. People are unlikely to attempt to work together to effect changes if they are afraid of one another and afraid of outside authorities. Likewise, in a fear-ridden situation, people are much more likely to define conflict situations as zero-sum games, where one party's gain is the other's loss, rather than as integrative conflict situations from which each party may gain.

In this type of atmosphere, people are likely to define situations in such a way that the appropriate mechanisms for influencing decisions of those in authority are seen as manipulation and pressure. That students in our secondary schools are learning this lesson well is evidenced by the large numbers of them who believe that other people cannot be trusted and that governments cannot be trusted. It is also testified to by the frequency of student protests that have been occurring in the schools; for what is a protest incident (at least in the majority of cases, where a school-related issue is the focus of the protest) but an attempt to pressure school authorities to take a position they appear to be unwilling to adopt otherwise? And at the conclusion of Chapter 4, we noted that the most significant learning outcome for SG participants is increased cynicism.

We are not suggesting that this problem of fear, in its more extreme forms, afflicts all secondary schools in Ontario. But the questionnaire responses we have received (especially comments written in by students on the survey forms) and the many interviews we have held with students, teachers, and administrators have convinced us that it is a more widespread phenomenon than most school authorities care to believe.

Overcoming this problem of fear with its attendant mistrust, cynicism, manipulation, and pressuring of others cannot be accomplished through modest structural alterations – for example, by making the student government more formally representative, or by adopting a house system. Nor is it likely to be overcome simply by expanding the range of decision areas over which students may have some influence; for if the atmosphere of the school is not changed, both students and staff are likely to continue to define such situations as zero-sum games.

What we are describing is substantially a human relations problem. A principal, it is often noted, sets the tone of a school. It is upon him that the responsibility for changing the school atmosphere falls. We have no quick and easy recipes for principals, although in the course of our discussion we have cited some examples of productive behavior in specific situations. More systematic training of administrators (and teachers and students) in leadership and group dynamics might be helpful; but such training probably should take a form different from that now available. The Ontario Ministry of Education, as well as some school boards and a private foundation (The Friends of Zak Phimister Foundation), have for some years offered courses and workshops in these areas. In our questionnaire to principals, we asked whether the principal, vice-principal, SG adviser, or SG members had attended any such training sessions. We compared the responses of teachers and students to some 87 other questionnaire items from those schools in which such training had or had not been received. In no case were any significant differences found. Whatever impact such workshops or courses may have upon the individuals who take them, the effect does not appear to spread out to the school as a whole.

While there is no indication that leadership or group dynamic sessions have had any impact on the school as a whole, there is also no evidence that any school has ever attempted to resolve the complex problems of interpersonal relations through intensive and sustained use of such sessions or courses. No school in our sample has initiated activities directed toward acknowledging and dealing with the variety of fears, and other feelings, that are present in the school. Even if such efforts should occur, it seems unlikely that they could fully succeed unless it were also recognized that some of the negative feelings result, not from poor interpersonal relations, but from certain organizational characteristics of the school system. What seems to be required, then, is a twofold approach: a willingness to deal with problems of interpersonal relations in a manner that stimulates the development of trust and openness in human relationships, and at the same time permits an examination of, and alterations in, systemic components of the school system – that is, the school, the board, and the Ministry.

If, for example, a particular principal's unwillingness to design appropriate learning experiences for student development of decision-making skills is based on his feeling that SG members are indifferent, this may be a matter between the principal and his student government. We have often told student representatives from particular schools that we feel most SG members are indifferent to what goes on in the school, and many of them have agreed. When the discussion has been pursued, however, several of these students have said, "Well, what's the use in trying to change things around here. The principal never listens to our ideas anyhow."

It seems likely that what some principals believe to be indifference on the part of the student government (or students) is, in reality, despair. And it is a despair that has every possibility of transforming itself into cynicism – certainly about the possibility of changes in the school, and perhaps about the flexibility of organizations in general.

The problem is that the principal hears the students saying, "I couldn't care less about what goes on in this school," and the students hear the principal saying, "I don't care what you have to say. It's going to be done my way." In reality, however, many students are saying to the principal, "We would like to become involved, but we feel you have no trust in us; that you won't let us try anything new or even discuss our ideas with you." And often the principal is really saying, "I would like to have you students become involved but I feel you simply don't care about the school."

The first step toward a solution is to get the messages straight – a difficult but necessary achievement.

Sometimes a principal may be reluctant to provide students with decision-making authority because of the possibility of negative repercussions. His fear of reprisals from higher authorities may be perfectly rational and adaptive; and in this case what is required is an alteration of the reward structure. If the boards' reward system inhibits rather than reinforces student learning, then there is something radically wrong with that reward system. This characteristic of reward structures has been recognized at the university level for some time – an example is the publish or perish syndrome, which tends to reinforce university professors engaging in scholarly writing while ignoring their teaching obligations. This problem has not been completely solved; but it is recognized, and alternative reward structures are currently being tested in a number of universities. No such experimentation appears to be occurring, however, in the school system of Ontario. Indeed, in many respects, particularly in organizational form, schools and school boards are extremely homogeneous.

This homogeneity stems in part from the establishment of rigid criteria that seek to guarantee uniformity between and within school boards. Such uniformity has been rationalized on the grounds that quality education must be made available to all Ontario students and that the best way to accomplish this end is to apply the same standards to all jurisdictions. The zeal for uniformity has, however, imposed a high degree of organizational rigidity on schools and boards, which in turn has inhibited much of the creative potential of principals and teachers, as well as directors of education and trustees. It has also made experimentation with new forms of school and board organization extremely difficult.

In 1949, when J. G. Althouse delivered the Quance Lecture on the *Structure and Aims of Canadian Education*, he said:

A high school that treats its senior pupils exactly as it treats its beginners is an abject failure, for the aim of the school is not to train pupils to follow promptly, accurately, and even willingly a prescribed code of behavior. The aim is to develop young adults who may be depended upon to cope courageously with the problems of life as they arise.[23]

In order for a large, modern high school to meet the objectives set forth by Althouse, it is necessary for principals to create new organizational forms within the school. This is a difficult task under the best of circumstances, and it may be an impossible one unless external constraints are relaxed or removed.

Theorists in the domain of decision-making have long recognized that decision-making has affective as well as cognitive components. Our feelings as well as our thoughts dictate our decisions. Thus, if educational decision-makers are to establish an environment that will permit the young to develop their own decision-making skills, it is necessary that they deal with their feelings as well as their thoughts, resolve problems in the interpersonal domain as well as the systemic, and teach the young by example as well as by design.

We began this book with a description of the surprisingly widespread and growing student protest movement in Ontario. It is perhaps appropriate to close on the same note. If such changes as we have suggested are not made in Ontario's schools, we can only conclude that Byron Massialas' account of the options open to students in the United States will continue to hold for our own secondary school students:

> We know from the work of Mark Chesler and others that participation in traditional-type school clubs and student bodies does not make much difference in the operation of the school. What really makes a difference is organized political action on the part of the students that results in political confrontation, political negotiation, and political compromise. The evidence from the schools and universities suggests that direct action tactics are quite effective in changing both the tempo and the direction of decision-making in the schools.[24]

This is not a vision of the future that is likely to appeal to those who are responsible for, or who live within, the secondary schools. But unless fundamental changes are made in these schools, the only likely alternative will be for even more students to drift into the indifference and cynicism that already characterize far too many of them.

Notes

1. Ontario Department of Education, *Living and Learning*, Report of the Provincial Committee on the Aims and Objectives of Education in the Schools of Ontario (Toronto: Ontario Department of Education, 1968).
2. *Programme of Studies for Grades 1 to 6 of the Public and Separate Schools* (Toronto: Ontario Department of Education, 1937). As a curriculum guide, this document has been superceded by other Ministry documents.
3. Ontario Department of Education, *Living and Learning*, p. 71.
4. *Ibid.*, p. 70.
5. Ontario Department of Education, *Recommendations and Information for Secondary School Organization Leading to Certificates and Diplomas*, Circular H.S.1 (1972/73), p. 5.
6. Byron G. Massialas, ed., *Political Youth, Traditional Schools* (Englewood Cliffs, N.J.: Prentice-Hall, 1972), pp. 2, 3.
7. M. Kent Jennings and Richard G. Nierni, "Patterns of Political Learning," *Harvard Educational Review*, XXXVIII (Summer, 1968), 443–67.
8. Maurice Gibbons, "Walkabout: Searching for the Right Passage from Childhood and School," *Phi Delta Kappan*, LX (May, 1974), 598.
9. A. B. Hodgetts, *What Culture? What Heritage? A Study of Civic Education in Canada* (Toronto: Ontario Institute for Studies in Education, 1968), p. 70.
10. *Ibid.*, p. 78.
11. *Ibid.*, p. 116.
12. Cited in Kenneth L. Fish, *Conflict and Dissent in the High School* (New York: Bruce Publishing, 1970), p. 171.
13. R. Duncan Luce and Howard Raiffa, *Games and Decisions: Introduction and Critical Survey* (New York: John Wiley and Sons, 1957).
14. Fish, *Conflict and Dissent*, p. 50.
15. *Ibid.*
16. *The Man in the Middle: How the Urban Secondary School Principal Sees His Role and Responsibilities* (Toronto: Canadian Education Association, 1971), p. 43.

17. *Ibid.*, p. 42.

18. This is not the actual name of the department. It does, however, describe the basic functions of the department being discussed.

19. We know of one case in a Metropolitan Toronto school where students under the guidance of teachers built a bleachers and there were no objections from the unions.

20. *The Man in the Middle*, p. 16.

21. Revised Statutes of Ontario, 1970, *The Schools Administration Act*, Chapter 424 as amended by 1971, Chapter 90, 21 (2), p. 17.

22. This feeling partially explains why anecdotal reports to parents usually consist of nothing more than platitudes or inane remarks.

23. Quoted in Ontario Department of Education, *Living and Learning*, p. 71.

24. Massialas, *Political Youth*, p. 247.